Praise for *Li*

'Sam Johnson-Schlee is a virtuosic c:
and Freud. It's impossible to feel the
how you furnish it after reading this ~~~~~~~~ ~~ ~~~ ~~, astounding
book.'
– Olivia Laing

'*Living Rooms* is fascinating, and beautifully written. I learnt so much
from it, including about my own tastes, since the book links up
domestic space and objects with culture, class, history, and politics in
such deft and illuminating ways. I loved this gorgeous and original
book.'
– Katherine Angel

'A beautiful book tracing the ideational, historical and material
origins of homes that Sam Johnson-Schlee has known, and of
familiar images and practices of homes and home-making from
renting in cities through the 2010s. *Living Rooms* places home and
home-making at the centre of a re-imagined world.'
– Aurelia Guo

'Marvellous, brilliant, and charming. You won't ever look at your
living room in the same way again.'
– Amelia Horgan

A catalogue record for this book is available
from the British Library

First published in 2022 by Peninsula Press

400 Kingsland Road

E8 4AA

London

peninsulapress.co.uk

Cover design by Tom Etherington

Typesetting by Geethik Technologies
Printed in Great Britain by CPI Group (UK) Ltd, Croydon

2 4 6 8 10 9 7 5 3 1

ISBN-13: 9781913512194

Living Rooms

Sam Johnson-Schlee

PENINSULA PRESS, LONDON

For Galvey

OPENING

The fruit flies were everywhere and I never really understood why. I'd tried to keep my studio flat clean: what were they eating? When it was time to leave I tidied up and tried to clean every surface. But when I moved out and the landlord and the administrator from the office where I worked came to make their inspection, they stood in the middle of the room and looked around disapprovingly. There must have been too much left, too much of my presence marked upon the surfaces. My residue was probably what was feeding the fruit flies, keeping them floating around in the shaft of light from the full length window which opened onto a balcony where sometimes I would smoke cigarettes.

The flat overlooked a courtyard that was hidden from Rue Oberkampf by large wooden doors, the kind which could be opened fully to allow in cars or vans. I imagine they were designed to let in carriages delivering goods to the ateliers on the ground floor, or to take away the products of the businesses that once filled those spaces. Now the ground floor was mostly converted into stylish homes. My flat was one of the many studios and one-beds that spiralled up one or another of the stone stair-cases whose iron balustrades led up from the courtyard.

My landlord had a Bengal cat who would peer outside, but this was an indoor animal. There were some children who occasionally got hold of a cache of bangers and would set them off one after the other. Most days when I got back from work I wheeled my bicycle past a group of people drinking Agrum, menthe verte, or grenadine. People would appear on their balconies to hang out their laundry or to smoke. Some evenings I would hear my upstairs neighbour having sex. I would go out for fresh bread in the evening and eat it with supper, then toasted for breakfast, and as a sandwich for lunch. And then on the way home another fresh *tradition, s'il vous plaît.*

I was trying to finish an MA dissertation and to stave off boredom. I was twenty-four. I'd arrived in the Paris of-fice of the marketing company where I worked expecting they would have something for me to do. Instead I played chess for hours and read about the coalition government, austerity, and rioting. You were not supposed to leave the office until the bosses did. In the evenings I curled up on the bed and read, or played computer games, or worried.

I think about this studio when I read Walter Benja-min describe a 'manorially furnished ten room apart-ment' in *One Way Street*; I compare my little Parisian flat to the grand interiors of the nineteenth century. Benja-min found something menacing in the plush velvet of the upholstery and the positioning of the ornaments. Like a camera, or a fossil, the interior captures a record of the life lived within it. To the attentive observer the life of an apartment's inhabitant can be read from the merest trace. Because of this Benjamin identified the apartment of the nineteenth century as the birthplace of the detective novel. Attuned to the vagaries of the model bourgeois interior, the great Victorian detectives like Auguste Dupin and Sherlock Holmes could scan its surfaces and read exactly what had taken place there.

While my little Parisian apartment was very different from those that occupied the minds of Benjamin and Dupin, it too was full of clues left by a body trying to escape the world. At the end of the tenancy the landlord and the administrator arrived in my room like consultant detectives. All of the detritus of my life that was invisible to me was glaringly apparent to them. I was guilty as sin.

I did it, I confess. I have ended each tenancy standing openhanded in the centre of a room: I LIVED HERE.

The spaces we separate out for living in are valuable only when they appear to have always been vacant and waiting for their new inhabitant. Each rental or sale advert is an essential fiction: like pretending to a new lover that you never really loved anyone else before.

But there is always a trace. Next time you move in somewhere and find that drawer full of instructions and spare things: empty it all out on a table. Have you been left a message hidden in plain sight? Does that fold in the fridge instruction booklet indicate an agitated reader trying to understand the reason why their lettuces are frozen and their milk sour? Was that lightbulb bought in error? Was that mark left by soup? Why is there a car manual in here?

The things that remain are clues: dust, scratches, Blu Tack marks, errant instruction booklets, expended batteries, holes. Don't be too quick to view your precursors as criminals. These are bits of their lives. How cruel to hate people for leaving behind evidence that they were there. After all, these pieces of stuff suggest wrongdoing only because of the collective illusion that it is reasonable for places where life takes place to be owned, and that they can be owned by someone whether or not they use them for their own life.

It is so widely accepted as to appear natural that the places where we dwell are commodities that can be exchanged on the open market or borrowed for a fee. Fluctuating house prices appear as if they were the outcome of a weather system too complicated for us to understand. Each estate agent is a genius of reading prices and fortunes. Inviting you to step into the interior of the commodity, they point out the cryptic signs that justify its price and explain how your life will be improved by acquiring the right to inhabit this space, however briefly.

Then some weeks later you arrive in the empty rooms, accompanied by nothing except a contract proving your right to be there. Standing with all your cardboard boxes around you inside an empty shell. Calcified layers of paint in an empty room appear suddenly like dead bone, not decoration at all. What to do? How do you find a way to affix yourself to this carapace and make it your home?

A few weeks after renting a small ex-council, one-bedroom terraced bungalow in South London, and still we had no doorbell. It was a dark winter evening, and Rebecca and I had been married a month. We invited a friend for dinner but forgot all about it while we argued about the state of our home. We were angry because we could not see how we could ever live there. Katia knocked, trying to raise our attention, but we did not hear her. When we eventually let her in she explained that she had been unable to miss our furious row. Realising that we were in no state to entertain, Katia decided to help us organise ourselves. She set out a list of tasks which we would complete in twenty-five-minute periods with breaks in between; she gave up her whole evening, I'm not sure we ever served the meal we had promised.

We needed to attach ourselves to the place, to distract from the cold walls with books, pictures, shelves, and furniture. With our boxes unpacked we could settle our lives into a kind of permanence, even as we knew that our landlords could whip the security from underneath us at any minute, just as the previous ones had done. We made the decision to damn the deposit and put up shelves and pictures all over the house. We spent days drilling holes and constructing flat-pack furniture. We ate lunch in Ikea three days in a row. Katia had unleashed a frenzy of settling. That spring Rebecca would grow vegetables in the garden; we ate tomatoes and courgettes all summer.

Fabrics, furniture, picture frames, plants, and textiles: what are all these things? The objects and designs of the interior are protective charms that fortify us from the world outside; they are the nesting materials that we use to hold ourselves in place inside the unwelcoming shell of a commodity. The boxes of things we had dragged there with us felt like a burden until we used them to fashion a home for ourselves. With the help of Katia, an interior that had felt so impossible on that winter night had been transformed into a place for living, all by the grace of a credit card and the hope of future earnings. But as ever, we were in a fantasy; our being there was not predicated on life but on rent. We had become the involuntary stewards of someone else's riches.

For Benjamin, writing about the bourgeois home of the nineteenth century, the home was an escape from the conditions of life in capitalist society. Yet this sets up a cruel logic that continues into the present: you work so that you can afford a place where you can forget how horrible it is to work. Added to this is the grim reality that those with the worst working conditions must work hardest for the lowest pay, and subsequently endure the least secure housing conditions. The home is a sanctuary, but it is also a trap.

It is odd to be able to walk around inside a commodity – there are not many commodities that one can step inside – but the secret of their value is no more visible as you walk around it. Homes, like all commodities, are treated as if their price on the market were integral to them, as if a property could not help but be worth what it is. But the truth of commodities, as Marx has explained, is that they harbour a social relation: that the value we attribute to them is derived from work that one person has done and another person has profited from. The allure of a commodity like a house is ultimately due to the work that produced it: this is what Marx referred to as the commodity fetish.

A house is presented as a righteous reward for the hard work of the person that owns it. This is an illusion that allows us to forget that the work of the labourers who built the house was not rewarded in proportion to the value it produced for the developer. You try to find a place to recover from life under capitalism only to end up in a shell made of a stranger's exploitation.

What else is there to do inside the home but to try to pretend that we do not live in such a bind? The things that we surround ourselves with are the props and scenery for a fantasy: the dream of a world beyond the conditions of everyday life. Floral fabrics mean we are never separated from nature. Sofas create a state of super-position between life and death. Picture frames are portals to the people and places from which we are separated. Pot plants embody the will of life to exceed its container. Woven materials hold us in a permanent embrace as if we were loved. And all together we may read the interior for what it is: a dream of a world beyond the limits of the commodity.

Our sleeping dreams are made of fragments and memories drawn from our daily lives, what Freud calls the 'residues of the day', which provide comfort and enclosure for our sleeping mind, though we may struggle to identify the meaning that lies behind their arrangements. We furnish our homes with similar fragments. But while on one hand our homes may appear to say something about ourselves, for the most part they are made up of commodities made of other people's labour. Where our dreams are made from pieces of our own life, our homes are fantasies made from pieces of other people's lives.

Like dreams, homes can be read as a kind of displacement; we create a space of relative isolation, but we do so through the ownership of commodities. In this way we weave ourselves into a web of social relations that extends across the world. It is easy to see in a child's drawing: you stick it on your wall to hold that person symbolically close to you. It is harder to see the same desire for intimacy in the furniture we buy to comfort our bodies. But I think that it is there, and that we might see it if we interpret the living room as if it were a dream.

*

I keep drifting off mid afternoon and walking into dream rooms. I enter one, a large glossy-surfaced open plan kitchen, and leave it through another door into the deep-pile living room of a childhood friend. Then a William Morris parlour, then the soft edges of a Jugendstil dining room, then the velveteen sobriety of Mrs Hinch's living room, then I am walking around the chimney and hearth of a burned-out house.

But I always return to a house made of wood where I lived from when I was about five years old until I was twelve, and where I have visited again and again throughout the rest of my life. The house is a bungalow built from a kit by my grandmother's maiden aunts. It is a dry-as-tinder, shingle-clad beauty extended by my grandparents by attaching a kit for a church hall onto one end.

Galvey – as it is called – was built in the garden of a neighbouring house. It has trees growing all around it and a wild hedgerow hiding it from the road. My mum's parents lived here after they retired, and when my parents separated, my brother and I moved here together with my mum, Emily.

Galvey has been constantly adapted to meet the needs of my grandparents as they have aged. At various points my grandfather, a painter and a glutton for light, has cut new windows and doors through the house. Its gradual dilapidation is also adaptation, it ages, it tires, and it is cared for by its inhabitants even as they become older. They keep telling us, 'All of our friends are dead', but their home is forever inviting new people in. At Thanksgiving (my grandmother was born in America) we stretch a table along almost the whole length of the studio and fill it with guests. My grandfather stokes up his wood-burning stove and the air shimmers with warmth radiated by bodies and hot cast iron.

My grandmother has the most beautiful room to write in. It is part of the house that used to be a garage. In between the kitchen and the writing room is a larder, a sink, space for a washing machine and a small electric oven for when the stove is turned off in summer. It is also the place where bee-keeping equipment was kept when they had a hive, so we called this space the honey house. When they moved to Galvey my grandmother and uncle put the bees in the back of the car, donned full bee garb, and drove for over an hour along the motorway out of London. There is also a toilet that I am not allowed to call a toilet; when my grandfather would open his studio to show his paintings he would put a sign up on it saying 'W.C.', and it would usually stay there most of the year until the next open studio took place. On the back of the door there was a broom handle with a small piece of wood nailed to one end so that you could thread toilet rolls onto it: a solution designed by my grandfather – but I don't know to what problem.

The writing room has bookshelves on all sides and a view to the garden with a window seat. When you walk in, to the left are the fiction shelves, to the right plays and poetry as well as various books about classics and classical sculpture. Also stored here are files and folders with various research materials in them. Like the folder that says MONSTERS on it with research for a lecture she once gave to an adult education class. Opposite the door to the house is a desk that has been moved here to make more space for my grandmother's large adjustable wheelchair.

When I was a child I would go in when she wasn't there. Everywhere around the room and in all the drawers were objects of great fascination, an articulated snake made from metal, a plaster cast of my uncle's head, a replica cuneiform tablet with a recipe for a toothache remedy made by my aunt. Nothing was better than going into her desk for staples, Blu Tack, paper clips, carbon copy paper – stationery which somehow always promised so much but never delivered. All around the desk she keeps drawings of her grandchildren, most of which we made of ourselves or of each other at various points in our childhood. Over the years I have had so many conversations with her in this room; its odour is distinct from the rest of the house and wherever I am I can summon the powdery dry smell. I love going in to her study to find her asleep at her desk, to tell her that there is a small glass of whisky waiting for her and a dish of peanuts to mark the end of the day. Head fallen forward, adrift mid-sentence in one of her dozens of notebooks.

Plants growing through walls, pets that both belong to them and don't. Galvey is both immaculate and ramshackle and it is here more than anywhere else that has shaped the interior that I dream of. As I write I walk through it again and again, opening the door to the sound of the cow bell tied to the handle and examining each room. Every part of the house is marked and imprinted by the lives that have been lived there. My grandparents seem to have a disregard for the value of their house; they have never really tried to remove the traces of life that have been lived here. Galvey is a record of years, it is a family member, and it is its own memoir.

*

Why does Galvey hold my attention like it does? Taste or aesthetics are not particularly useful ways to engage with the interior. Each person finds objects which have an allure for them, and this allure is not easy to decode because, I think, it refers to something hidden. In *Swann's Way*, Proust's narrator describes this well:

> Suddenly a roof, a glimmer of sun on a stone, the smell of the road would stop me because of a particular pleasure they gave me, and also because they seemed to be concealing beyond what I could see, something which they were inviting me to come and take and which despite my efforts I could not manage to discover.

17

Proust's narrator is kept awake by the weight of meaning behind each object he observes, yet he cannot reach what lies behind them since he finds that objects are always reluctant to reveal to him 'the thing for which they themselves were merely a cover'.

Across the seven volumes of *In Search of Lost Time* Proust expands the world of his past almost endlessly into sentences that gather like velvet slipping from an upholsterer's work table into voluptuous folds. Proust's narrator returns again and again to the house in Combray, as if looking for something:

> The air was saturated with the finest flour of a silence so nourishing, so succulent, that I could move through it only with a sort of greed, especially on those first mornings of Easter week, still cold, when I tasted it more keenly because I had only just arrived in Combray: before I went in to say good morning to my aunt, they made me wait for a moment in the first room where the sun, still wintry, had come to warm itself before the fire, already lit between the two bricks and coating the whole room with an odour of soot, having the same effect as one of those great country 'front-of-the-ovens', or one of those chateau mantelpieces beneath which one sits hoping that outdoors there will be an onset of rain, snow, even some catastrophic deluge so as to add, to the comfort of reclusion, the poetry of hibernation; I would take a few steps from the prayer stool to the armchairs of stamped velvet always covered with a crocheted antimacassar; and as the fire baked like a dough the appetising smells with which the air of the room was all

curdled and which had already been kneaded and made to 'rise' by the damp and sunny coolness of the morning, it flaked them, gilded them, puckered them, puffed them, making them into an invisible palpable country pastry, an immense 'turnover' in which, having barely tasted the crisper, more delicate, more highly regarded but also drier aromas of the cupboard, the chest of drawers, the floral wallpaper, I would always come back with an unavowed covetousness to snare myself in the central, sticky, stale, indigestible and fruity smell of the flowered coverlet.

In this sentence (one sentence!) the narrator finds so much satisfaction in the unremarkable. His memory of this ordinary room is transformed into a delectable parcel made of folded layers of pastry containing delicious morsels of furniture. I read this and immediately I am four years old and pulling the cotton throw from the pink Habitat sofa in my home in Norwich while waiting for the food and the attention of my mother and reaching my arm into the depths of the upholstery to find what? a coin, a crumb?

And I am still looking in the upholstery, still reaching my hands in between the cushions looking to discover the secret that makes these objects and spaces so alluring to me. Perhaps it is pure sentimentality that places Galvey at the heart of my domestic dreaming, but I think there is more to it than that. Worn thin by familiarity, the boundaries of the commodities which make up this home seem to reveal more than others. Is this hidden thing a glimpse of the social? Of the ties that bind the lives inside the house to those outside? After all, every object that we encounter is the product of someone else's labour. Hidden inside our homes is a powerful truth: our lives depend on one another; we live because of the work of others. In this sense the home is a site of both isolation and attachment. Life under the alienating logic of capital might be described as being alone together.

During the coronavirus pandemic I found myself not wanting to be inside and not wanting to be outside. Someone recommended to me that I try leaning out of the window. In *Fierce Attachments*, Vivian Gornick describes how she escaped the airless atmosphere of her family home the summer after her father died:

> I began sitting on the fire escape in the spring, and I sat there every night throughout that immeasurably long first summer, with my mother lying on the couch behind me moaning, crying, sometimes screaming late into the night... I found I could make myself feel better simply by swinging my legs across the windowsill and turning my face fully outward, away from the room behind me.

The space in between inside and outside is a very good place to think. In *Strayed Homes* Edwina Attlee includes the fire escape among her examples of the home spilling out from its private domain and into the public sphere. Fire escapes 'show the envelope of a building to be permeable in a way that is not quite appropriate'. Age fourteen with her back to her mother, Gornick was able to begin to separate herself from that apartment and her family. Here with her face full of the night air, her 'magical isolation... became a conduit for waking dreams'. Somewhere between the hostility of the outside and the cloying succour of the inside, there is a place where another world becomes possible.

The dreamlike world that Gornick finds on the fire escape is something that I find for myself as I shuttle between the interiors that come to me while I snooze on the sofa in my study. By paying close attention to these fantasy rooms I find myself on the edge of waking and deep sleep, somewhere between inside and outside. Sometimes being inside is like being asleep, but if I try to shift myself towards wakefulness, I begin to find the deeper desires that are fulfilled by the interior. Swinging your legs onto the window ledge is a kind of critical thought.

In my home I can become temporarily oblivious to the horrors of the world outside, held fast by the comfort of soft furnishings. Freud argues that every dream is motivated by wish fulfilment. The simplest are 'comfort dreams' motivated by physical need: one goes to bed thirsty and dreams of pouring oneself a glass of water. And yet according to Freud our dreams also fulfil other, wilder wishes – those buried in the unconscious – wishes that have been distorted and repressed; in order to understand them, it is necessary to interpret our interior life.

By looking closely at the places where we live, we can wake up to the dream we don't always know we are sleeping through. If we read the clues of the domestic interior, then I think we might find a glimpse of another world: one beyond the alienation of life under capitalism. Perhaps the primal wish that drives the work of making a home is not to become isolated but to find attachment. As you walk around your home, pay attention to the clues that, as Freud says, have been 'left over from the life of the day'. As with the dream, there is a deeper truth discernible beneath the sometimes incoherent and misleading patterns you observe on the surface.

CHINTZ

A more manorial ten-room apartment for me please. Bored of living in this century, I think I will redecorate. I am my own magic lantern, projecting onto my room new patterns and decorations, new furniture and ornaments. Like the entertainment laid on for Proust's sulking narrator, my wish projector can replace 'the opacity of the walls with impalpable iridescences'. Another interior to replace the stubborn, uncooperative walls I live within. Let all the surfaces in your room waver and be replaced with something else.

Dense vines with birds hopping from branch to branch and animals climbing between leaves and reaching out their paws. The plants growing over my walls and furniture are ready for harvest, every branch heavy with fruit, and yet, impossibly, in many places they are flowering at the same time. My room is a miracle, a microclimate where everything can be alive all at once and all together, any day of the year.

Beginning to feel that the room is my own, I stand up and rearrange the soft furnishings. I adjust a doily so that it sits just right, I brush a little dust away from the glass case where my stuffed owl lives. I take a large bed covering and lay it out on the divan; taking hold of it by the two corners of one of its shorter sides, I throw my arms up and at once the large decorated palampore is filled with a bellyful of air and slowly drops to the bed. I even it out at the corners so the design sits centrally, then flatten it out with a sweep of my hand. The fabric is densely woven and smooth to the touch; the work of dyeing, fixing, painting, printing, and washing have made it supple and light. Spreading its branches out towards the edges is a large flowering tree growing from the rocky ground. And flowers everywhere! Great blousy peonies, open-mouthed flowers with haloes of small petals, monstrous orchids, anemones, dahlias, sprays of cornflowers. At the base of the tree are two peacocks with their heads turned upwards admiring the boughs.

I am an imperial lordling, admiring my chinoiserie from my divan and dreaming of the Eastern limits of the colonial world, wilfully oblivious to the plunder, violence, and death in distant places that my desire for grandeur has funded. Here I am, a lost duke, washed up on the Rue Oberkampf, dreaming of the Orient.

*

Before chintziness there was chintz, a fabric produced in India and imported to Europe by colonial traders. Indian chintz was all the rage in the seventeenth and eighteenth centuries. The bright colours were made with plant-based dyes and mordants. This required a detailed knowledge of the properties of plants and minerals: blue from indigo, red from maddar, yellows from pomegranate skin and turmeric. Each colour was attached to the fabric by co-lour-fixing chemicals derived from myrobalan fruit and iron or alum. Complex patterns were produced in multi-ple stages of painting, printing, resist dyeing and mordant dyeing. The finish, the quality of fabric, the colour-fast-ness – all this added to the desirability of chintz. Indian textile workers were masters of a technique that was im-possible to replicate in Europe.

By the seventeenth century chintz textiles were ex-tremely fashionable. When Samuel Pepys's wife was deco-rating in 1663, she chose chintz fabrics to adorn the walls of her study. The popularity of the fabric was perceived as such a threat to European cloth manufacture that British and French governments introduced tariffs, and later out-right bans, on the import of Indian printed cloth lasting well into the eighteenth century, and it was only when Europe was able to undercut the cotton-weaving industry of India that the legislation was gradually lifted.

The flowers and plants that decorate Indian chintzes are not always easy to identify in nature. They are visions of trees growing from rocks and bursting with multiple flowers, or endlessly winding vines, or bright uniform sprigs, or ripe fruits. Their colours tended to be deter-mined by the pigments and chemicals available rather than by any actual botanical referent. It is thought that styles and patterns developed through exchanges of ideas and motifs along Indian trade routes with the Middle East, China, and Japan.

Botanist Deborah Metsger writes, 'Artists combined morphological features – or their sense of them – from a range of different flowers and leaves, and embellished them to create hyper-real flowers and fruits.' There is something ecstatic in the cloth-flora of Indian chintz. Bright and unfading colours which are worked into woven cotton by workers who have mastered every capacity held by the raw materials.

Chintz conjures another world. For Europeans this was a generic orientalist exoticism. 'Chinoiserie' was often used to describe the decorative products that arrived to Europe on boats from 'the East'. But these visions belong to the workers who designed them, not the householders who buy them. For them the dream of chintz was not of distant places, but of the immanent world of work transformed into a site of endless bounty.

When George Washington died in 1799 there were 317 enslaved people at his Mount Vernon estate in Virginia; their labour had been used to renovate the house, to farm tobacco, flax, hemp, cotton and grain, and to run the home and the estate. Some years earlier, he and Martha had chosen fashionable Indian and European fabrics to decorate Mount Vernon. One room contained block printed wallpaper with a botanical sprig pattern, while a large bed was hung with multi-coloured botanical designs. Outside their wealth was produced by slave labour, inside the Washingtons sheltered in an Eden that did not belong to them.

Chintz fabric was at the heart of a controversy involving the Washington family's enslaved seamstress Charlotte. She was accused of wearing an expensive Indian chintz dress which had been stolen from a white Virginian ferry owner and sold on. The fact that a black enslaved woman wore such a fashionable item caused much consternation, as its previous owner, one Mrs Maciver, considered the Washingtons' seamstress undeserving of such fine garb.

The history of chintz is entangled with the racist violence of enslavement. Cotton grown by enslaved people on plantations, like the one where the Washingtons lived, made it possible for Europe to take over the production of cotton cloth from India. The labour stolen from enslaved plantation workers enriched the capitalists of North America and Europe, leading to a drastic expansion of the bourgeoisie, while cheap raw materials fuelled the production of the imitation chintz that was used to decorate the homes of this ever-growing social class.

The science of botany helped make all this possible. One of the purposes of botany was to develop new methods for farming plants like cotton in order to increase European control over raw materials. Accordingly, the triumph of European printing techniques and the mass production of imitation chintz brought the imposition of European botanical empiricism onto the chintz aesthetic.

My street in Paris, Rue Oberkampf, was named after Christophe-Philippe Oberkampf, the French industrialist who mastered the production of printed calicos. His factory in Jouy-en-Josas gave its name to a style of printed cotton which is still used today: toile de Jouy. In 1795 Oberkampf started to produce a cloth decorated with flowers from around the world, each one directly taken from the pages of an encyclopaedia produced by the botanist Jean-Baptiste Lamarck. Unlike the floral excess of the flowering tree, these tightly packed leaves and petals bring to mind a botanical collection. The extravagant dreams of the Indian chintz artist have been brought to order by European industry and empire.

It was at this point that chintz began to signify something other than a fine Indian cloth. As imitation chintz flooded the market, the word slowly became an indicator of cheap and fussy decoration. In 1851 George Eliot wrote to her sister to describe some fabrics she had considered buying as being too 'chintzy'. The industrialists of industrial Europe had overcome the threat posed by Indian textiles. But as patterned cloth became a product accessible to more Western consumers, it began to lose its fashionable sheen. Chintz became chintzy, and instead of lauding Indian craft the word now derided European industry.

It was a kind of trickle-down effect: the fashions of the Victorian bourgeoisie collected in the corners of the working-class homes of the twentieth century. 'Chintz' became a useful way for the middle classes to distinguish themselves from the frilly aesthetics of those parts of society they viewed as backwards.

When I was growing up my dad's parents had a home that might have been called chintzy. My dad's mum was born to traveller parents but settled when she was still young. Her husband, my grandad, was a farm labourer and factory worker. Their home was a storeroom for a dream of a different relationship with the world, a universe pieced together trinket by trinket. I remember the potpourri in a little gilt-edged pot on top of the toilet in their bungalow. I remember the bronze-cast figurine of a horse in their sitting room, the antimacassars, the por-

celain figurines, the silver picture frames, the shortbread
that came in a Constable biscuit tin.

My grandparents had placemats decorated with reproductions of seventeenth-century inn scenes: shouting men,
dogs rolling on their backs, roast meat. One Christmas I got
a big jar of marbles and we tipped them out in the kitch-
en all over the laminate floor made to look like flagstones.
Everything in that house seemed to be reaching towards
another Essex: a pastoral world where people simply lived
among things, where the labour of a farm worker was a
sweet and easy pursuit and there were plenty of places
for stopping and resting, like that little boy in Constable's
'The Cornfield' who drinks from a stream while his little
dog watches the sheep. In their tastes, my working-class
grandparents took the Victorian bourgeois dream of rural
life and made it their own. They were constructing a utopia
from bits and pieces, a place where they could summon
their family to their side with a glance and where the rural
and the domestic were a seamless continuum.

My grandparents loved to walk, to watch birds. At
the end of their garden was a field full of horses that my
grandfather would call over for us to see more closely: the
man, who was otherwise so quiet, could speak to horses,
and he could make anything from wood. My dad's parents had a secret command of the landscape where they
had never had power. As they grew older a hard life of
exchanging their labour for a fraction of the value they
produced for capitalists eventually gave way to a pleasant
and quiet life of walking and sharing binoculars.

They'd waited a long time for a crumb of comfort. They
decorated their house with echoes of Victorian bourgeois

life, a dream of what it might be like to own the means of production, for the places where they walked to be common land and the products of agriculture shared according to need.

The reproduction pastoral scenes on my grandparents' walls were originally commissioned by landowners who wanted to represent their holdings on the inside of their homes. But do not dismiss the interiors of their home as some kind of cultural impoverishment. Their home was not decorated in homage to the lives of the ruling classes, but in resistance to it. They were not meekly imitating the rural gentry but demonstrating their own right to the countryside that they knew more about than any landowner. I don't know what they would make of me writing this, I didn't know them as well as I could have.

When the working class inherited the household aesthetic of the bourgeoisie they got to imagine a society where property ownership dissolves. Displaying the trappings of the rich highlights that this wealth was stolen from the poor in the first place. Chintz allows every home to appear to be the dwelling of a landowner, and if everyone owns it then nobody owns it. The tree of life, a common chintz motif, is an image of life exceeding the limits of its environment, a vegetal revolution whereby from rocky ground grows a tree that can produce any kind of flower it wills. Maybe chintziness has become an unconscious reach for the commons: first we will inherit the landscape paintings through cheap reproductions, and next we will take our part of the land.

*

In the 1990s housing had firmly shifted from utility to asset. It was now terribly naïve to treat your house as a place to live when it might instead be a means to make money. In the UK this was the culmination of a number of policies from the Thatcher government: Right to Buy, which was the final nail in the coffin of the post-war idea that the state should de-commoditise the housing market via universal housing provision, and the 1988 Housing Act which, among other things, shifted power in the favour of the landlord in rental agreements.

By the middle of the next decade, being a landlord was no longer the preserve of the few, and had become an investment opportunity for anyone with the capital required for a deposit. Like the de-regulation of financial markets in the early 1980s, the de-regulation of the property market provoked a furious acceleration in activity: houses succumbed to the logic of the market, and within a few years they were transformed from places to hold life into places to hold value.

It was at this time that the annihilation of chintz became an imperative. Doilies and floral sofas presented an existential threat to this new era. Displaying one's attachment to a house was foolhardy, properties were to be commodities of frictionless exchange. To be seen to aspire towards the aesthetic of stately homes and grand Victorian townhouses was now terribly gauche. Chintz had long since become a catch-all, a byword for blousy frou-frou, a florid aesthetic of nicknacks. Now it was a loaded signifier of class aspiration.

Laura Ashley florals and fussy ornaments were the endpoint of an aesthetic trickle down from Parisian apartment, to stately home, to middle England, to council or ex-council house. The British class system has long enshrined a disgust for 'social climbers' who adopt the cast-off trappings of the rich. By the nineties, the high fashion of the Victorian interior lived on in the pathetic grandeur of Hyacinth Bucket, the lead character of *Keeping up Appearances* (1990–95), a sitcom whose central joke was the audacity of a working-class woman acting as if she had inherited wealth.

Against the backdrop of privatisation, it was time for middle England to adopt a more efficient aesthetic, one that better suited a society where perpetual ascension of the property ladder was expected to resolve every problem. Entire television programmes were dedicated to encouraging people to erase themselves from their own homes. Chintz was too personal. Neutral tones allowed the market to keep working, magnolia meant that a house was always ready to go onto the market.

By the end of the twentieth century, streets of Victorian terraces built by industrialists who sidelined in social engineering had been transformed from functional containers for working populations into rows of investments made of brick. When they were built they would have had back gardens with privies and wash houses to enable a more modern and hygienic way of life. Later they will have been subdivided and rented out. By the 1940s, with the city emptied out by war, they may have been the kinds of places where a single person could rent a room in a bedsit. In the sixties partitions will have been knocked through and small extensions built to create space for modern amenities.

By the nineties the people who had bought these houses for little more than what they earned in a year will have seen successive decades of appreciation. Today streets like these in Hackney, Walthamstow, Peckham, or Brixton occupy a place in the housing market that is accessible only to the extremely wealthy. If this street is in Notting Hill, Fulham, Chiswick, or Hampstead they may have had their basements excavated and extravagant glazed extensions built in the back gardens to maximise their footprint.

It was on a street like this that Ikea chose to film the iconic 1996 advert that called for Britain to 'chuck out that chintz'. The ad featured a faux-protest song where someone trying to sound like Shirley Collins sang over scenes of women revolting against their old-fashioned homes, and presented chintz as a regressive menace.

The advert starts with a skip being lowered into the middle of the road. Women are shown ripping down curtains and doilies and coming into the street to get rid of them. An animated sequence shows a woman heaving huge stone letters to replace the word FRUSTRATED with LIBERATED, while in the background we hear 'We're battling hard and we've come a long way, in choices, in status in jobs and in pay'. Chintz isn't simply outmoded design; it is everything that is holding back the lives of British women. Namesh Ramachandi, the copywriter for the advert, called it an act of 'propaganda' which set out to 'convert the UK's sense of what homely is. To get the Ikea style adopted, they had to put it right at the centre of British taste, and push out the old version of British taste.'

Chintz once stood in for the glamour of 'the Orient'. But in its umpteenth iteration it had lost any hint of the exotic. The Ikea advert played on a class hatred that derided any pride and pleasure taken in the home by people who were deemed not to be keeping pace with modern Britain. Ikea was selling an image of ease and brightness in contrast to the glowering stuffy interiors signified by floral bedspreads, pelmets, and doilies. The song beseeches the nineties householder to liberate themselves – or *her*self – and to embrace modernity: 'Our homes could be playful and happy and light, loose and informal and stripy and bright, let's use our resources, let's muster our forces, to fight chintz-oppression with bold self-expression!' This gendered incitement to revolution ends with a veiled threat: 'Don't let that doily go on and spoil everything, chuck out that chintz today!'

This Ikea advert came out one year before Blair's New Labour government came to power on a campaign that abandoned the working class and focused instead on promises of progress and wealth for middle England. The chintz battlements that had created the tchotchke castles of the suburbs were rejected along with the Conservative government. In their place came the low-friction, open-plan environments that, three decades on, still dominate the bourgeois imagination of what a home should be.

In a study of home magazines from 1922, 1952, and 2002, Martin Hand and Elizabeth Shove developed an account of the transformation of the British kitchen. At the beginning of the century it is a space where women are promised an optimisation of domestic work through labour-saving devices, by the fifties the kitchen is dominated by a fantasy of streamlined modernity, and by the noughties the space hides all evidence of work and becomes the centre of the everyday life of the home. Today the ideal home remains a site of illusory ease, a space that can be wiped clean of the residues of living and which does not allow chintz's flowery dreams to take root.

Chintz was an aesthetic of residues and accretions: keepsakes, knickknacks, trinkets, baubles, doodahs, gewgaws. The home was a place of security where protective doilies were designed to protect the surface of the furniture and every object sat on top of another object. Draped materials and floral patterns created an organic excess: fleshy and intimate. Your objects were your archive and your legacy; it was your trinkets and furniture that were the investment, not the shell you lived within. By the nineties Ikea was necessary because even the comfortably well off did not have enough money after buying their house to furnish it with expensive things.

In the nineteenth century value was held primarily by objects; however, by the nineties the value of furniture was negligible compared to the value of the home. As houses became assets many times more valuable than the average annual salary it was immodest to make them your own, and the open plan interior was designed so that the crime of living in the interior of a commodity could take place without leaving any evidence behind.

*

The chucking out of chintz foreshadows New Labour's eviction of the working class from the labour movement.

In the nineties we were told that every man wanted his Mondeo and every woman her breakfast bar. The third way and Ikea turned their back on a century of domestic dreaming.

One of the perennial features of the chintzy interior are the floral prints of William Morris. As socialism was being banished from the arena of electoral politics, so, too, were the floral prints that Morris had dreamed would bring art to the homes of the working class.

William Morris wanted a society where there was an unalienated relationship with the landscape, and where the decorative arts would be a pleasure that everyone could afford. My dad's parents were awarded a little microcosm of this in exchange for a long and quiet working life. My grandfather had a beautifully organised woodworking studio where he made furniture; together, he and my grandmother went for walks in local RSPB reserves and admired the wildlife. But this was a facsimile of the kind of life that they should have always had access to.

Morris's botanical prints give a glimpse of his utopian vision: wallpapers and upholstery undulating with living vines. Morris had seen what could be achieved for the very wealthy through the decorative arts of weaving and wood-carving. He had seen that it was possible to escape the limitations of the interior through art:

> To turn our chamber walls into the green woods of the leafy month of June, populous of bird and beast; or a summer garden with man and maid playing round a fountain, or a solemn procession of the mythical warriors and heroes of old.

Morris wanted to bring the decorative out of the bourgeois interior and into the homes of the working classes; he believed that the joy of decorative fantasy should belong to everyone. Morris imagined that the urban working classes living in slums and shared rooms in sub-divided terraces might be able to challenge the limits of their interior through decoration. Chintziness was a way of tearing down the edifice of the commodity from the inside, disappearing domestic containers by giving the urban working classes a view of an idealised landscape. Like the dream images conjured up by Indian chintz makers, Morris's leafy fantasies were a reminder of the world they deserved to live in but had been denied.

Although he was nostalgic for the production methods of the past, Morris nevertheless saw the capacity of machinery to create new kinds of design, and he hoped that the machinery of capitalist production would make the beauty of traditional handcrafts accessible to all. Prefiguring Walter Benjamin's 'The Work of Art in the Age of Mechanical Reproduction', Morris argued against attempts to create an illusion of the artist's hand in mechanical designs. The artist should exploit the specific ability of the medium to produce complex patterns:

> The more and the more mysteriously you interweave your sprays and stems the better for your purpose, as the whole thing has to be pasted flat on a wall, and the cost of all this intricacy will but come out of your own brain and hand.

Morris saw that in the decorative there was the opportunity to transform walls from mere barriers into a space to think. Their very flatness is an opportunity for speculation, the interwoven mysteries of their design transforming surface into landscape.

None of this is to say that design alone can transform the conditions of our lives. Today decorative goods are a way to ameliorate the brutality of commerce with the gloss of taste. Morris would feel both awe and devastation on entering the gift shop of any stately home to find the avalanche of Morris & Co pattern mugs, mouse mats, calendars, diaries, glasses cases, and tote bags. He was under no illusion that the market could benefit the arts; he knew how the most optimistic of artistic endeavours could yet find itself 'crushed to death by the money-bags of competitive commerce'. Art, as Morris saw it, was incompatible with capital. Paraphrasing John Ruskin, Morris said that 'ART IS MAN'S EXPRESSION OF HIS JOY IN LABOUR'.

But there is a secret in the commodity, however alienated the workers who made it: it conceals within it a seed of social relations. As Marx's concept of the commodity fetish reveals, the objects we covet are valuable because they are made by human labour. To make the labour of production visible in the object, as Ruskin and Morris hoped to do, is an act of subversion, it reminds us that the product should remain in the gift of its producer, and not the capitalist who exploits them.

When Proust read Ruskin he found himself consumed by his way of engaging with the objects and materials of culture. Perhaps Proust's conviction that there is something behind our immediate encounters with manmade objects – some secret 'thing for which they themselves were merely a cover' – is drawn from Ruskin's conviction that the beauty such artefacts contain is derived from labour. While joy may be dwarfed by the indignity of exploitation, there is something social hidden within objects; what Marx calls the 'social hieroglyphic'. Could it be an unconscious desire to be in relation to others that makes the commodity so alluring to us?

*

As the category of chintz expanded, its meaning came to incorporate lacework. Runners, cushions, antimacassars, curtains, bedlinen. In the toilet, in the dining room, in the bedroom, in the living room.

According to Ikea the most menacing of all of these is the doily. At my paternal grandparents, doilies always heralded the arrival of a biscuit or a cake. The grand ornamentation of lace protects surfaces while adding froth to everyday occasions like sitting down to eat lunch. Why such disgust for lacework? As with floral fabrics, it was at the point that the working class could indulge in the frilly pleasures of lace that it began to be reviled by bourgeois tastemakers.

Lacework has its origins in intensely wrought production methods. It was an extraordinarily expensive product, and even as the industrial revolution allowed the manufacture of lace at scale, it still required the work of the hand.

Most of the workers involved in making lace in the nineteenth century were female, and many of them were children. However, that lace-making was a feminised form of labour did not mean that the working conditions were any kinder. In fact usually quite the opposite. In 1900 Emily Jackson wrote a book about lace-making (her other books included histories of toys and silhouette portraits) that lists, in seven points, the advantages of the lace industry in England.

1. Women need not leave their homes in order to do the work.
2. In a properly organised lace school the girls are well cared for and protected while learning the industry.
3. Perfect hygienic conditions and personal cleanliness are essential for the lace-maker.
4. There is plenty of scope for individual effort and distinction, a stimulating consideration, which puts the lace-worker on a superior footing to the woman who merely works a machine.
5. The work is so light that the most delicate woman or girl can undertake it.
6. Mastery of the technical details is so easy that in lace-making countries, such as Belgium and Italy, children of seven or eight years commence to learn the 'stitches.'
7. Every woman newly employed in lace-making is one taken from the great army of women who in earning their living, encroach upon those trades and professions which have hitherto been looked upon as the monopoly of men.

Lacework was the ideal form of labour for the disciplining of women. The women who made lace could stay in their homes; they could exploit their 'light and delicate touch'; it kept them clean; it was easy enough for children to do; and it prevented them from taking jobs from men.

This is the way lace-making was imagined to function by those with the money to buy handmade lace from Honiton in Devon, or any other of the lace-making centres of Europe. It is as if the lace simply emerges from the women that make it like a sigh. Lace is a product which embodied a domestic ease and grace with which the bourgeoisie could embellish their homes and their clothes.

Even after machinery took over much of the manufacture of lace it remained entwined with the domestic. Lace finishing and mending around Nottingham and Bedford employed thousands of women and children in their homes, where their health and safety fell outside the purview of industrial legislation. In *Capital* Marx claims that of the 150,000 people employed in lacework in Britain, 140,000 carried out work in private homes and informal sweatshops. In 1861 one in eight of all women working in lace in the Nottingham area had tuberculosis. Marx cites the *Children's Employment Commission* from 1864:

> The average age at which the children start to work is 6 years, but in many cases it is below 5. The usual working hours are from 8 in the morning until 8 in the evening, with 1½ hours for meals, which are taken at irregular intervals, and often in stinking workrooms... But in those finishing sties there are between 67 and 100 cubic feet for each person. At the same time the oxygen of the air is consumed by gas-lights.

In Honiton, where children and women were employed to make pillow or bobbin lace, they often worked in so-called 'lace schools' run by older women in cottages. These workplaces, which were often foul from the lack of air circulation and hygiene, employed children as young as two years old.

But for the bourgeois homeowner, on the other hand, lace was a further layer of comfort and protection, an interface between object and object, furniture and person. My dream furniture is protected from scratches and stains by lace doilies, each one an intricate pattern of entwined leaves and flowers. They soften the edges of things, they add to the fortifying layers of textile that shield me from the outside world.

Of course the thing I am escaping – the slow violence of a time and space dominated by capital – is exactly what brought these ornaments into existence. But the cruel working conditions are not evident to me when I place a crystal cut vase full of peonies onto the centre of my doily mat on my sideboard. I try to escape work by amassing one thing after another to hold me in place. Little do I know (or maybe little do I care) that each thing is a fossilised imprint of somebody else's stolen labour.

In *Fierce Attachments* Vivian Gornick recalls her neighbour Nettie, whose name seems chosen for a lacemaker. Nettie is a young widow with a child, whose sexuality and dreaminess play a central role in the young Gornick's early encounters with the world.

Nettie has worked in a lace factory but now makes lace from her home. She works while Gornick sits at her table and together they engage in exchanges of fantasies: for Nettie it is always a rescue by a wealthy benefactor or the revelation that she is an heiress; meanwhile Gornick imagines herself as a speechmaker and a revolutionary. The snatches of joy that Nettie is able to find in her labour inspire fantasy scenarios where she escapes the limits of her everyday life.

In a moment of waking dream on her fire escape, Gornick is watching a woman, whom she eventually learns is a sex worker, walk up and down the street in wrinkled nylons. The young Gornick conjures an image of herself somehow being able to heal this woman. She imagines herself wrapping the woman in 'some lovely material' at once warming and healing. Gradually as Gornick sinks further into her vision she recognises the material as the lace made by Nettie. Then in her vision she sees all three of them together:

> All of us with our faces laid sadly against small pieces of lace. Not a mantle of lace for any one of us, only these bits and pieces and all of us sorrowing against these bits and pieces.

It is the lace that brings them together, but it is also fragmented. They are together not in joy but in sadness, though something of the acknowledgement of this sadness is healing for each of them. The little pieces of lace are slipped in between them, their lives held in tension as the fine threads that bind them measure the distance between them and the potential flash of their solidarity, were it ever to be realised.

*

The genius of capitalism is to make you pay for objects which help you to escape it. It may feel intuitive that the commodities that we possess say something about ourselves, but the source of their exchange value is always only the exploited labour of the workers who made them. In capitalism everything you purchase is a fragment of the labour of people you will never meet. The dreamiest chintz, the most breath-like doily, or the blandest Ikea place mat – all these are crystals made of other people's work. At the end of the Ikea ad a doily is snatched from beneath a lamp and thrown out of the window as if to dispose of something liable to explode. The treacherous doily is a tacit acknowledgement of the commodity fetish: the echoes of handwork that persist in its frills make the doily an incendiary device closer to being sparked into life than your average unadorned Ikea place mat.

Then as now the chain of social relations embodied in each of these objects of desire is full of violence, alienation, cruelty, hunger, and death. Unconsciously we try to piece back together the time that we have had taken from us by employers by acquiring objects produced by those that we will never know. The sinister triumph of both the third way and Ikea was to sell us the lie that commerce can deliver liberation. An open-plan kitchen with a suite of modern appliances *might* save a little domestic labour for a middle ranking ad executive in Tooting; but however free its smooth surfaces might appear of the human labour that created it, it comes at the expense of labour elsewhere, happening far away, to other bodies.

'We've come a long way', says the Ikea advert. It is a telling phrase. The modern illusion that we have liberated ourselves from the economic and social conditions of the past is in large part a consequence of having exported those conditions around the world. Out of sight, out of mind. Around the same time that Ikea was demanding that British households chuck out their chintz, it was embroiled in a controversy relating to the use of child labour in its supply chain. A 1994 documentary broadcast in Sweden showed children and families at carpet looms, forced to work without pay in order to clear debt. The conditions of the factories where Ikea rugs were produced recall the chapters in *Capital* about the conditions of work in nineteenth-century industrial Britain.

Ikea sought to save its reputation by working with the UN and Save the Children to investigate the extent of the problem with its South Asian suppliers, and a new code of conduct promised that improvements would be made. But with a supply chain that flails across the globe, the problems recur. Even if we accept the best intentions of the business, they are operating in a system which relies on the exploitation of labour for profit: the very point that New Labour decided to forget as they tried to usher in the third way.

In an extensive report published in 2014, Siddharth Kara documents the extent of abuse in the carpet weaving supply chain in India. He demonstrates that retailers including Ikea are buying from suppliers who force indebted workers to weave carpets in appalling conditions. In the regions of Uttar Pradesh and Madhya Pradesh, Kara and his researchers found villages where workers were drawn into debt slavery with financial advances that entire families would have to work off at wages as low as

$0.11 an hour. With no way to escape their debt, workers supplying retailers in the United States with handwoven rugs were working six or seven days a week.

I think that chintz has something more to it than the frictionless aesthetic of open plan living. Not because the commodities rely any less on exploited labour; they don't. But because it leaves a clearer set of clues linking life inside the bourgeois home and the lives outside that are exploited to furnish it. The secret of the commodity is just that bit easier to see in chintz, the fact that each commodity is produced by another person just a little closer to the surface – that bit harder to ignore. It is as if chintzy commodities cannot quite contain the lives that are wrung out in their production. The tree of life on the big palampore, bursting out with undisciplined blooms of all kinds; the fantasy fronds that twine through one another as if reaching into the warp and weft of the calico itself; the doilies making haloes for every vase or place setting as if to show that this quiet object is full of life.

Perhaps this is why European chintzes such as those made by Oberkampf tried so hard to contain nature in the rigid taxonomy of botanical drawings. To prevent it from getting loose, to stop the life of chintz from ripping through the walls of the apartment. When Ikea called for the end of chintz it heralded the triumph of the landlord – of a home which makes life invisible, where no residue may be left that might reduce the value of the property. From now on there was to be no hint of the labour that produced the things that fill our homes, nothing to indicate the presence of a hand in the production of clean blank surfaces.

There is something deathly about the bourgeois interior and the chintzy middle England home; as Benjamin says, elaborate ornamentation closes off every means of escape as if one were in a tomb. But the chintzy interior is also a dream of a living room that really *lives*. In the chaos of trinkets, in the frills and folds of lace and floral upholstery, the furniture replicates the interdependence of the natural world. Every object rests upon another one, every surface is willing to give a little to make room for a companion. A pastoral fantasy which not only dreams of threads of connection woven between non-human flora and fauna, but between the humans who shelter among the furniture.

William Morris did not believe that socialism would be brought about by verdant wallpaper, but he did think it would allow a glimpse of a different life. The traditional, the artisan, the decorative – in all these, there is a vague hint of another relationship between human lives. Chintz carries with it an echo of a past before each person was (in the words of Marx) ripped 'loose from the umbilical cord of his [sic] natural species-connection'. My dad's parents looked back to an imaginary before-land in their Constable biscuit tins; but like Morris they were also looking in the direction of utopia.

VELVET

'Girls only want one thing and it's a living room with hardwood floors a green velvet sofa and a colourful rug.' Since I read this tweet I see green velvet sofas everywhere. I am pursued by emerald plush: in magazines, television programmes, on Instagram. Now I want one, I suddenly feel that I have never wanted anything so much, a slumpy, slightly baggy couch which holds me just how I want to be held. And then, oh! When I finally swing my feet from the sofa to get up to find a snack, then I want my socks to land in a shaggy carpet to massage my soles for one step, two steps – and then here is the sweet slippery sensation of socks on a parquet floor.

I like to run my hand this way and that over plush materials to see the traces I leave behind. And soft cushions – feather ones please – the kind that breathe out when you drop onto them. A sofa that loves you back. Cushions should not be a nuisance, they should support your head when you lie full length, or prop up your knees. Sometimes I just like to hold one. I knew someone who used to say 'hold me' during lulls in conversation, it was always unsettling but I know what he meant.

If I am sitting on a sofa I do not want my thighs to change shape. The cushions on the base of the seat should be deep enough and soft enough that your thighs stay nice and round. In other words – I want upholstery that is softer than my body.

A colourful rug. It depends on the rug, it depends on the colours. I can bring to my phantom foot the sensation of all manner of rugs. The almost silky, velvet pile of an expensive Persian number, a bouncy carpet-feeling kind of rug, one with bright coloured abstract shapes, it is on a white painted floor. I want an Anni Albers rug, the colours running interference across the floor, breaking up the certainty of that hard plane. I want the *Red Meander* from 1954. Linen and cotton, a labyrinth losing its way across the floor. I would trace the path of it one foot in front of the other while I talk on the phone, while I watch television. With a bad back I will lie flat, I will do corpse pose, I will follow instructions from *Yoga with Adrienne* on this rug.

All this will be on top of my parquet floor, little pale rectangles, in need of wax, scuffed up but still slick. The herringbone pattern: one vanishing point after another, wood turned into stitches. The surface always folding in on itself, where is all that geometry disappearing to. I will slide across this parquet in my stockinged feet as I race to answer the door until one day I slip and land hard on my coccyx and my head smacks on the floor (I'm fine). Oh! To gasp as you drop your coffee cup (don't smash, don't smash) – is there just enough kindness in the timber to forgive the stoneware handle? Maybe this time. Jumping on the pool of coffee to absorb it with my socks before it reaches Anni's rug (not this time, Satan).

The enveloping sofa, the play of geometry, the colour, the slide, the scuff, the bouncing coffee cup. This is a living room.

*

I like my environment to be very upholstered. I prefer to be horizontal, to have my legs straight out ahead of me and my back held by soft furnishings.

When my maternal grandfather was a young man he put an advert in the paper that read: 'Wanted: 7 foot sofa for a 6 foot loafer.' The reward for this pithy classified was large and white with soft feather cushions.

Most days he would take off all of the cushions and beat them and puff them up until they doubled in size. Then he would toss up the blanket and let it float down, tucking it in between the arms and the sofa cushions. Seeing it like that, it was too much to bear, particularly when we knew that guests were coming. All I wanted was to dive onto it and hear my body force out all the air suspended in the feather stuffing.

As I grew older and taller I became more useful to family members who wanted to escape the monstrous embrace of this sofa. After an evening drink my mother would hold out her arms so that my brother or I would help her lever herself back into the world. My grandfather is ninety now and if there is something that needs fetching from the kitchen he will shift a little as if he might go himself until someone younger offers. Once he has sat down, it is not easy to get up again.

I like a sofa that is so comfortable it makes me forget about my body. Like sensory deprivation a good sofa suspends time. This is what I want when I am trying to escape the outdoors: a sofa that is a pocket universe where I decide how time passes, where time does not equal money and money does not equal time. Outside, my life slides like a cog into the machinery of work; outside, when time passes I am either working, or late, or wasting time. Laying out full stretch on the sofa I think I know something of the certainty of death. I escape the outside world into the comforting oblivion of the sofa.

Patients on Freud's couch were encouraged to put their feet on the furniture. Freud would sit behind them at the head of the couch and listen intently to the stream of free association. Lying on the couch is like being in parentheses. A space for forgetting in order to remember. Outside time and space and between wakefulness and dream, the sofa is the perfect place for the analytic work of recollection.

Dreams themselves have something of the sofa about them. What Freud called 'dreamwork' is a kind of labour undertaken fully prone, asleep and held by soft furnishings. But more than that, dreams are the culmination of a search for comfort – malleable, distorted, compressed, displaced. Like the domestic interior, dreams are the product of an unconscious effort to transform the things we fear into something more manageable.

Freud's patient Sergei Pankejeff, known as the Wolf Man, is famous for a dream about wolves. In the dream he wakes up in bed, the window flies open and outside he can see a tree. On the tree are six or seven white wolves. In his drawings of the tree the branches are bare and spread left and right, and there are no branches reaching towards the boy and the window. The wolves' ears are pricked up, reminding the Wolf Man of an image of Little Red Riding Hood from the front of a book that his older sister used to frighten him with. The wolves have long bushy tails, more like foxes than wolves, which hang below the branches or are otherwise flicked upwards.

Freud traced the origins of the dream to a primal scene in Pankejeff's childhood. He was ill and sleeping in a cot in his parents' room one afternoon when he woke up to see his parents fucking doggy style. This moment of admiration and desire for his father became entangled with other images: his nanny walking ahead of him and saying 'look at my little tail', his sister and that book cover, his grandfather telling him a fairytale. All these things together in the sleeping mind of a child exposed castration anxiety and a desperation to be the passive recipient of his father's admiration and love.

The Wolf Man's dream consigns to the outside something disturbing which happened inside. It apparently displaces a scene of bedroom activity between familiar humans into a vision of static and strange animals on the other side of the threshold. By consigning this memory to the outside the boy is able to consider it again, this time from the safer position of his own bed. Like the sofa from which he recounted the dream to Freud, the bed allows the boy to reconsider something which has been troubling him.

For Freud the couch was a site of productive alienation. It was a tool for coaxing traces of memory buried deep inside his patients' unconscious. But I'm not sure Freud always attended to the psychodrama of the interior itself. It is an odd blind spot as his own rooms were full of elaborate decoration. In his memoir the Wolf Man described the place where he sought treatment:

> The rooms themselves must have been a surprise to any patient, for they in no way reminded one of a doctor's office but rather of an archeologist's study. Here were all kinds of statuettes and other unusual objects, which even the layman recognized as archaeological finds from ancient Egypt. Here and there on the walls were stone plaques representing various scenes of long-vanished epochs. A few potted plants added life to the rooms, and the warm carpet and curtains gave them a homelike note.

Like an archaeological site, his couch was made one layer at a time: a simple wooden frame divan built up with cushions and then covered with a carpet made by the nomadic Qashqai people of Iran. This sense of Freud as archaeologist was not unintentional. In *Studies on Hysteria* he compares the work of analysis to archaeology: exposing, layer by layer, the remains of a 'buried city'. Freud the intrepid explorer ventures beyond the frontier and into the psychic interior.

When Freud died there were sixty-five objects left on or inside his desk in his house in London. Ro Spankie calls these objects 'the dreamlike montage of associations and ideas that Freud surrounded himself with as he wrote'. In the manifold objects and fabrics with which he decorated his consulting room, maybe we see a reflection of Freud's own dreams. On the top of Freud's desk were figurines and antiquities from around the world. From his chair, on the far right corner of his desk Freud placed a statue of the Egyptian God Thoth. In Ancient Egypt the baboon god was believed to weigh your heart after death in order to ascertain the goodness of your life. Freud liked to stroke Thoth like a dog while he thought.

Opposite his desk is the chair he sat on at the head of his consulting couch. It is a single seat armchair set on elegant wooden legs. It looks snug; there are two cushions, one to sit on and one to support the back. It looks ideal for sitting on for a long time without becoming sleepy. Predictably it is upholstered in green velvet and set on a parquet floor, a large rug stretching out in front of it.

Freud's home appears as if it always anticipated its future as a museum. In these objects he leaves so many traces of himself, enough to create his own buried city in a permanent display. The London home in which he died is now called the Freud Museum, and people go there to view the vast collection of objects with which Freud decorated his interior in the hope of learning something about him. Each of these objects seems carefully chosen to record something, and each bears the trace of his touch.

Freud neglected the furniture when he delved into the Wolf Man's interior. And he neglected the politics of being inside for such a privileged child. Pankejeff had come to Freud because of an unshakeable depression which he described as feeling as if he saw the world from behind a veil. Freud traced this back to the Wolf Man's birth; he was born with his caul intact: a hermetically sealed gift. Perhaps the wish at the heart of the dream was to escape the cloistered life of an impossibly rich young child.

In the pictures that Pankejeff painted of his dream, the tree does not look like a real tree but a symbol of a tree. At some point in his analysis Pankejeff suggested to Freud that the trees may in fact be Christmas trees, that the wolves were like presents hanging in the boughs. In a memory of Christmas around the time of the dream, the Wolf Man recounts being furious because despite having a birthday at Christmas he had only one allocation of presents and not the double allocation he felt he deserved. Already a member of the elite, Pankejeff was anxiously acquisitive.

When he was around five years old the Russian countryside was wrecked by famine. While the poor starved outside, he may have been quibbling over Christmas presents. This famine was an early flashpoint in the development of radical politics in Russia. Years later, Pankejeff's recovery from neurosis, the end of his treatment with Freud, and the October revolution would all come within a few years of one another. The Pankejeff fortune was seized by Bolsheviks in 1917, and he never returned to Odessa.

The primal scene, his parents doing it in the afternoon, the Christmas tree, the governess – whatever else it is, this is a story of a life lived oblivious to the outside world. In his memoir, the events that take place within the estate, within the menacing space of family, are much more threatening to him than the events that leave him penniless. Perhaps his wish was fulfilled when the wolves came through the window and tore apart the upholstery. Perhaps he could be freed from the claustrophobia of his childhood bedroom only when his wealth was taken away.

*

For the bourgeoisie in the nineteenth century the interior, with all its plush surfaces, represented both an escape and a trap. Layer after layer of artefacts offered a kind of protection, but also made a kind of prison. In *The Arcades Project* Walter Benjamin writes of the bourgeois apartment dweller:

> It encased him with all his appurtenances so deeply in the dwelling's interior that one might be reminded of the inside of a compass case, where the instrument with all its accessories lies embedded in deep usually violet folds of velvet.

For Benjamin the compass case represents both protection and a space formed to entirely enclose the body of its inhabitant. It is an idea which is at once monstrous and inviting.

The nineteenth century had been completely transformed by capital. Time and space had been consumed by the logic of property and work. Relationships between people were shredded by the transformation of life into value. Against this backdrop, the decoration of the bourgeois home was a place to seek comfort as if in a dream. The desire to escape the world and to reconnect with other people was displaced by increasingly intimate relationships between the bourgeoisie and the commodities they owned.

In Benjamin's archive there are three photographs, given to him by his friend Sasha Stone, that show precisely the type of bourgeois interior that he was writing about. The room that these pictures depict is stuffed with knick-knacks, doilies, patterned fabrics and wallpaper, mirrors, clocks, and ornaments; as Esther Leslie notes, in this 'opulently cluttered and cushioned space ... there is barely room between all the amassed things for its inhabitant.'

The wall is decorated with a floral print I can't quite make out, and hanging on it there is an array of carefully organised picture frames. There are tables, dressers, and whatnots, and on top of all this furniture are figurines and ornaments – some look like classical figures, others appear to be dancers. I think I can see two separate clocks, each one halted by the camera. There are table cloths and antimacassars with lace trim, some of the upholstery appears to be done with floral patterns, perhaps flocked. And huddled around the table, as if they were inhabitants of the room, are velvet armchairs.

The overall effect is to produce a space in which time slows to a trickle. This is a world outside the world where plush surfaces enclose the body. As Benjamin explains, all these soft furnishings, decorative fabrics, ornaments, and artworks were protective enchantments:

> Chairs beside an entrance, photographs flanking a doorway, are fallen household deities, and the violence they must appease grips our hearts even today at each ringing of the doorbell.

Patterns taken from across 'the Orient', heavy drapes, velour, satin, and upholstery moulded themselves around the body. Shut in to an enchanted space where wealth allowed the wealthy to pretend that the objects and materials they collected were valuable because of their inherent beauty and culture, that they were more than commodities. They were desperate to believe that these objects were enchanted with a remnant of less alienated life. In their embrace the apartment dweller could feel cared for, held, even loved by inanimate objects.

And yet if the bourgeois interior of the nineteenth century is a site of security, then it is also a site of death. 'On the sofa the aunt cannot but be murdered', says Benjamin; the comfort of the bourgeois apartment creates a feeling of life awaiting inevitable death. Velvet, a favourite choice for the lining of coffins, is perfect for such a moribund place. Today, this aesthetic survives only in funeral parlours and crematoriums, where deathly stillness is mistaken for an atmosphere of contemplation.

A masterful effort from the unconscious to provide us with succour: the fruits of other people's labour and exploitation are distorted to fulfil a wish for the bruised psyche of the bourgeois apartment dweller to be protected from the same structures of cruelty.

*

The Latin word *villus*, meaning shaggy hair or tuft, is the etymological root of the words velvet and velour. Velvet is a plush fabric; most accounts seem to trace its origins to the Middle East. Plush fabric uses looped thread to create pile. Originally in velvet manufacture the loops were cut, meaning that the surface of the fabric is made up of individual severed threads, whereas some cheaper plush materials (e.g. velour) leave the loops intact.

It is as if plush materials need to be touched. They are designed to receive the bodies and hands of the inhabitants whose homes they furnish. The sheen of velvet almost responds to your glance as you walk past and it catches the light. When you stand up from a velvet sofa it remembers that you were there. And in the most care-worn and long-lived armchairs the patches of threadbare material are a permanent record of the resting of arms and the leaning of heads.

Benjamin was fascinated by this ability of velvet to record contact: 'Plush – the material in which traces are left especially easily'. These are the clues that inspired the creation of the detective; for Benjamin the two go hand in hand. It is little wonder that Freud loved detective novels, particularly Sherlock Holmes; the ability to deduce motive from traces is the art of both the detective and the psychoanalyst, both are analysts of the bourgeois interior.

It was in *A Study In Scarlet* (1887) that Sherlock Holmes first put his magnifying glass to work. He is at a murder scene in an apartment off of Brixton Road: 'As he spoke he whipped a tape measure and a large round magnifying glass from his pocket.' He proceeds to carry out an inspection. Talking to himself and becoming increasingly oblivious to the people with him, he is absorbed by the minute details of the room:

> For twenty minutes or more he continued his research-
> es measuring with the most exact care the distance be-
> tween marks which were entirely invisible to me, and
> occasionally applying his tape to the walls in an equally
> incomprehensible manner.

Sherlock Holmes's scientific approach to detection is pre-
mised on the notion that everywhere people go they leave
traces of themselves. The interior of this South London
apartment contains a record of the murder that took place
here; and with the right method it can be pieced together
again.

Before Sherlock Holmes there was Edgar Allan Poe's
Parisian detective C. Auguste Dupin. Benjamin calls
Dupin 'the first physiognomist of the domestic interior.'
In *The Purloined Letter* (1845) Poe tells the story of a government official visiting the detective for advice. The official is concerned about a letter containing an undisclosed
scandal which had been stolen by an unnamed politician.
The police feel certain of the guilt of the culprit but cannot find the letter; they have searched up and down the
rooms of this high-profile politician, but the letter is nowhere to be found.

The police bring microscopes for inspecting chair
spindles and drive needles into the upholstery; but the
mystery remains. When Dupin asks the police how their
investigation is proceeding, he is not surprised to hear
that they have had no success. Similar to Freud, for Dupin
the art of detection is not only a matter of the applica-
tion of scientific techniques but of psychological insight.

Dupin inveigles his way into the house of the culprit, wearing green-tinted spectacles in order to hide the object of his gaze.

> At length my eyes, in going the circuit of the room, fell upon a trumpery filigree card-rack of pasteboard, that hung dangling by a dirty blue ribbon, from a little brass knob just beneath the middle of the mantel-piece. In this rack which had three or four compartments, were five or six visiting cards and a solitary letter. This last was much soiled and crumpled. It was torn nearly in two, across the middle – as if a design in the first instance, to tear it entirely up as worthless, had been altered, or stayed, in the second.

Of course this letter, so conspicuous in its inconspicuousness, is the one that has been purloined. It was concealed by a true master of the trace, someone who knew that the searchers would never anticipate that clutter could conceal the answer to such a secret. They were inspecting the spindles of chair backs when, all along, the letter was disguised as a letter. Only Dupin's intuition for the relationship between the apartment and its inhabitant could decode such a ruse.

Like in dreams, we cannot help but betray ourselves in the traces we leave behind in the domestic interior. Dupin is appalled by the actions of the police with their unsophisticated approach to the search for the letter. Less fluent in the grammar of the bourgeois interior, they are too direct. But when the French police search for the letter, looking inside every item of furniture, I wonder if they are looking for something different. Prodding and probing the furniture, perhaps they are zeroing in on the greater source of power, and the greater crime: the violence of capitalism, of stealing work and forgetting the worker you have stolen it from. The aristocratic Dupin cannot consider that there might be the traces of other wishes, other secrets, and other motives concealed within the home.

In the living room there is a kind of dreaming. Even as we embellish the interior with fragments and reflections of the things we dream of, we are also planning to escape the shell-like interior altogether. Benjamin again: 'the utopia has left its trace in a thousand configurations of life, from enduring edifices to passing fashions.' The dreaming that takes place in the places where we live is not just made from traces of ourselves, but from the traces of every body that has contorted itself in order to produce the commodities that decorate them. The bourgeois home is at once an individual trap and a collective dream. Inside the chair spindles, hidden deep within the upholstery, yet invisible to the microscopes and probes of the searching policemen, lies the residue of a thousand days unknown to us.

*

Mrs Hinch's home is a monochrome wonderland. Sophie Hinchcliffe set up an Instagram account to document her approach to cleaning in March 2018, and her account reached one million followers by October the same year. Scrolling through the images that she has taken of her home you'd be forgiven for assuming they were all taken in black and white. The engineered wood floors, the walls, the furnishings, the throws, the crockery, everything is grey. It is disconcerting, unreal – like a home viewed in a silvery mirror, a plush grey dreamscape.

On 26 March 2018, Mrs Hinch posted her first picture of the sofa. Grey floor, a deep pile shaggy rug, a grey cube footstool, a grey velvet chesterfield-style sofa, a silver-framed mirror reflecting back a grey wall and a chandelier, a curtain gathered with a tie with a long silvery tassel.

[house and tree emoji] #greyhome #greyinterior #cosy #interior123 #homesweethome #stairway #homeso-fig #interiordesign #silver #f4f #interiorfollowtrain #interiors #living room #livingroomdecor. #follow-4follow #interiordesign #antiquesilver ##dfs #fur-niture #crushedvelvet #kyliecurtains #woodflooring #whisperrug #greyhome #cosy #countryliving #essex #maldon #radiatorcover #fromhousetohome #cushions #mydfs #homeinterioruk

The house is presented as a site of utter composure, her velvet sofa displays no trace of having ever been sat on, not a mote of dust, the cushions stacked, the rug fluffed. The whole image is tilted towards the left so that the sofa appears to be at risk of sliding out of frame on the smooth floor. This is a polished jewel of an interior. The wildly askew camera angle means that the earnest intent of the photographer is laid bare: behind the camera is a person trying to squeeze in everything that she is proud of.

This traceless interior calls to me! Like my grandfather's sofa with pillows fluffed for a guest. I want to climb on the furniture, I want to roll in the pile of the carpet and try to squeeze out all the air from the sofa cushions. But the genius of Mrs Hinch's account is not in the photographs, but in the dozens of archived videos of the cleaning it takes to maintain the traceless interior, which are filed under the heading 'Hinching'.

Let me tell you, I hate to clean, but these videos! They are adventure tales starring a hand in a rubber glove: the pair chase dirt and grime around the house in double quick time. Her videos cut between shots more quickly than a reality TV show, and are interspersed with ecstatic moments like when she suddenly reverses time so that the sponge leaps from the bath of its own accord! With each beat the annotation of the video changes, she tells us the name of the cleaning product she is using, she offers an affirmation. At the sight of her newly tidied make-up drawers she exclaims, 'I hinched myself happy!'

It is as if Mrs Hinch wants to erase every trace of human life from the interior. In one sense she zeroes in on the abjection of the trace. Every mark left by life reminds us painfully of our icky embodiment. A nail clipping down the back of the sofa. A pubic hair in the shower, coiled and waiting. Cleaning like this is an attempt to eliminate death from the home, to stop time passing and hold everything in a permanent state of just right. Having been hinched, the interior is ready for its new owner. Imagine the frustration that the nineteenth-century detective would feel in such an interior, no clutter to hide among, no trace of life.

Right! Time for a quick Dusthunt!
You will need...
One empty handheld hoover [heart eyes]
And you need to...
HOOVER EVERYTHING! [Laughing face]

A hand lifts the vacuum cleaner like a weapon and moves towards the sofa. To the soundtrack of M People's 'Moving On Up', the powerful vacuum whines as Mrs Hinch, in voiceover, tells us, 'I love finding things in the sofas.' And then, to cap it all off, she tips out some of the vacuum's contents onto a piece of kitchen roll to admire her work.

It is easy to cast Mrs Hinch as a puritan. She, too, is a physiognomist of the domestic interior – but of a different type to Dupin and Holmes. Mrs Hinch understands the work behind the surface, she knows how the clues got there and she knows how to remove them. She does not only interpret but she commands her home. Poe, Conan Doyle, Freud, Benjamin – I doubt any of them ever cleaned a room in their life. Holmes would never have stooped to ask for advice from his housekeeper Mrs Hudson: she knew his methods, but he did not know hers.

Dupin or Holmes would have no hope against Mrs Hinch, their genius depends on their exceptional male attention to domestic traces. The banal details neglected by their arrogant peers are so obvious to them. But when the great detective arrives at this grey velvet home, every trace will be hinched out of existence. Nothing will remain to be magnified.

The secret of Mrs Hinch is not that she hates the traces that are left behind by life, but that she loves them. In her approach to cleaning this furious labour is cast as an act of almost ecstatic pleasure, she is not disgusted by dirt but she seems to cherish it. Silvia Federici warned against any notion that domestic labour is the loving duty of a woman, and of course this is true. On one hand there is something about Mrs Hinch's Instagram that feels regressive: the happy housewife et cetera... But on the other hand she is earning millions of pounds for her determined battle against matter out of place. Perhaps the popularity of the cleanfluencer is not because they show the world how to enjoy cleaning but because they are adequately paid for it. Every one of Mrs Hinch's followers wants a clean house, but they are also dreaming of wages for housework.

I want to be in a house that has been hinched and to roll my way through it. All a girl wants is a green velvet sofa, the infinite promise of touching and being touched. It's sexy. But more than that, look at how the cushions sit on the sofa, their different textures of plush, their warp pile threads reaching out for one another like two furry single celled organisms making contact with one another via waving cilia. All that static electricity waiting to jump from one thing to another.

The interior is read by the detective as a record of the owner. But when the traces and clues are stripped away we see how things relate to one another. The French policemen, whether they knew it or not, were looking for this secret when they probed the furnishings of the aristocratic letter purloiner. Holmes and Dupin can only solve crimes because of the bourgeois fetish for the commodity. The immaculate objects of the hinched interior are truer to the worker who made them than they are to the person who bought them; they have been restored to their factory state. The trick of the commodity is to convince us that it belongs to us, and to allow us to forget everyone who exchanged their labour so that we could have it. But when the trace is removed there is, in the palpable intimacy of two velvet cushions, a glimpse of social relations between things.

*

When the wind is blustery and it is overcast in central Scotland, the surface of Loch Leven looks like grey velvet. On the western side of the loch is an island, and on this island is the ruin of Loch Leven Castle. This is where Mary Queen of Scots was imprisoned for a year 1567–8. While there, she was forced to abdicate the Scottish throne in favour of her son James VI, and she miscarried twins who are thought to have been the children of her third husband, the Earl of Bothwell.

Mary was a devout Catholic, and English Catholics supported her claim to be the rightful English monarch. Elizabeth I recognised her as a threat to the English throne and arranged to have her arrested and imprisoned. In the National Museum of Scotland there is a wall hanging from the castle which is associated with Mary. It is red wool with appliqué black velvet, embroidered with gold thread. On the hanging are two panels, each with three floral arrangements arranged vertically. The panels are bordered with further elaborate floral designs capped by a broader piece of fabric, almost like a pelmet over chintz curtains.

The wall hanging is dated to the early seventeenth century, decades after Mary had left; but its decoration and grandeur seem determined to establish the legitimacy of her claim to the throne of England. The floral patterns consist of stylised thistles and roses representative of Scottish and English monarchs. The heavy golden embroidery is a display of authority; embroidered wall hangings like this were part of royal livery, rolled up and transported as monarchs travelled from place to place. In a painting by Daniel Mytens made of Mary's son James I & VI, once he had become the King of England and Scotland, he is seated in front of an extravagant embroidery, his throne on top of what appears to be a large Persian rug.

I mention all this because Mrs Hinch's sofa is named after Loch Leven. It comes from the Country Living collection made by DFS:

> Taking inspiration from some of the beautiful natural landscapes around the British Isles, these gorgeous sofas are handmade to order in our UK factories by skilled craftsmen, using quality fabrics crafted in Lancashire mills to create a range of timeless classics that will look stunning for years to come. As *Country Living* magazine editor Susy Smith says: 'The Country Living collection at DFS is for anyone who feels their heart is in the country.'

The grey velvet material that covers this chesterfield-inspired frame aims to embody the British countryside.

The sofa is the surface of a loch turned into furniture, it is the flesh of the union made into a seat. Now everyone with £1599 can have the authority and power that comes from velvet, once the preserve only of royals and courtiers. 'British made', by 'skilled craftsmen', the sofa is a dream of unalienated artisan labour. Like every aspect of the interior, it is a vision of something less brutal than the reality of life under capitalism. DFS promises to smooth the violent edges of the outside world and give you a sofa that you can love and that will love you back.

When *Country Living* was first published in America in 1978 it was dedicated to an aesthetic of Early American homemaking, and it was the fastest growing magazine on the Hearst Roster. It was launched in the UK in 1985, the era of Milton Friedman, of Reagonomics and Thatcherism – the market let off of its leash. In the midst of an economic revolution, people yearned for the aesthetic of primitive accumulation.

The founder of DFS, a major donor to the Conservative party, is also a board member for the Duke of Edinburgh Award, a scheme in which children go out into the countryside hiking and camping and carrying out charitable works. The Loch Leven sofa emerges from the same mythology: that we can balance out the rapaciousness of capital with an appreciation for the beauty of the natural world. There is something amnesiac about the dream of country living. It is a phenomenal act of displacement; I can't think of an easier teaching aid for the concept of the commodity fetish.

Workers made my green velvet sofa, just as they did Freud's psychoanalytic couch and the Wolf Man's bed.

A cotton-synthetic mix: cotton from India and rayon manufactured in Laos. Rayon is a material made from plant-derived cellulose that is treated with chemicals such as carbon disulfide, a neurotoxin that is known to cause early death among some of those who work with it. The hardwood frame is the endpoint of a wildly complex supply chain, some of the timber coming from the Baltic, some from North America; the wood is sawn into planks in one place, then planed and cut to size in another. Drivers, sailors, warehouse workers, wholesalers, salespeople, auditors, sustainability consultants; it goes on. The synthetic foam manufactured by a factory in the Indian state of Telangana from petrochemical-derived polymers.

Foam is the velvet of late capitalism. Designed to hold your buttocks, to take an impression; but unlike the bourgeois interior of the nineteenth century, it must be able to bounce back to its original state. Polyurethane foam is the product of chemical reactions designed to create uniform structures as the reaction produces gas and expands into a framework of bubbles. Its zenith is memory foam, a material whose name promises one thing but that delivers something very different. Memory foam, which emerges on conveyor belts in endless strips in factories across the world, is valued for its ability to forget the touch of its owner just as it has forgotten the touch of its maker.

And on: staples, nails, nylon thread, machinery involved in the manufacture, dyes, fire retardants, plywood, and on and on, and feathers, and metal brackets, and rubber casters. All these things coming together in a factory in Lancashire where a man boasts to a visiting interior design blogger that he can use his nail gun to attach the upholstery material over the carcass of the sofa in thirty minutes.

Thousands of hands touching every component of your sofa inside and out. Hours of work and hundreds of business owners taking profit from the surplus labour of every single worker at every single stage. But when it arrives in your living room I'd be damned if even Sherlock Holmes could find a clue that would lead him to the secret of the commodity.

PICTURE FRAMES

A few years before he died my dad's father walked my brother and me around his bungalow in Essex. After my parents were divorced we saw him and our grandmother less and less, and by the time we tried to reconnect she was in a care home because her Alzheimer's was so advanced. She wouldn't have been able to recognise us.

On the walls of the home where he now lived alone, my grandfather had dozens and dozens of framed pictures and photographs. In his bedroom one wall was almost entirely covered. Among these photographs were pictures of me and my brother along with all our cousins – school photographs which had been sent to them by my mother or her parents even in the years when we barely saw my dad's family. There were also pictures my dad, Trevor, had painted and drawn, a self-portrait he made when he was young, a detailed drawing of a bird.

My dad used to paint large abstract paintings. But he made pictures for his parents that were much more realistic. I suppose he painted and drew for them in the hope that they might understand where he was coming from. I don't think they could comprehend the world of abstraction where he spent most of his time, maybe no one could.

Walking us around his house I think my grandad was trying to show us the clues that he and our grandmother had pieced together about their distant grandsons. And that the wall space was shared equitably with pictures they kept of our cousins. After his death, my aunt delivered me a Sainsbury's bag for life with some of these framed pictures in. There was also a folder with loose photographs and one or two letters and Christmas cards from my mum's side of the family. One is a letter from my grandmother in 2001, it says: 'It makes me sad to think that you haven't seen Sam & Kenza at their new heights. Sam is as tall as I am.'

After my parents separated and my dad became disabled we more or less stopped seeing his parents. Now and again we would speak to them on the phone. They would pass it back and forth between them and we would try to speak loudly and clearly so my grandmother could hear (she wore a hearing aid). It was as if they were speaking from somewhere very far away. But that day in the bungalow I saw all the things they had done to make sure we were still in their homes, even though we didn't visit because my father was too unwell to take us. My mum's mum wrote in 2001: 'I wonder if there is any way that we could arrange a visit without putting you to trouble?'

Had I been a detective assigned to piece together the family life of my dad's parents based on their home, I would have taken the pictures on the wall at face value. These images would have told me that they had close and loving relationships with all their family and grandchildren. That they saw my father as much as they saw us, and that they were following our every achievement. Only later as I opened the box with the Christmas cards and letters from my other grandmother would the full story emerge. Each piece of correspondence was a gesture of solidarity and an admission of guilt. My mum's parents knew us and my dad's parents did not, at least not beyond our heights, ages, and school years.

With his gallery walls my grandfather had assembled his family life, he had given us our unearned place in the roster. I think he was telling my brother and me, without having to say so out loud, that we were never absent from their lives. The framed pictures conferred the truth of our existence but they misled about our presence in this home. I had never visited until then, even though it had long been within my power to do so; I had left it until my grandmother did not know my name and my grandfather was already dying.

Photographs have that power, to make us feel as if things that are far away are close. They are sort of like portals, the picture frame a door that stretches across an impossible distance. They are very useful for managing the things that are most present to us, as well as the things that are most absent.

I used to have a photograph of my dad in a walnut frame. It belonged to my mum, I think. Either I or my brother found it somewhere in the house. It was in my room for a while, later my brother had it, I'm not sure where it is now.

In the photograph the collar of his zip-up coat sits just right on the nape of his neck and his square jaw is stark in the black and white image. I can't say I ever knew him like this. He is looking off into the distance somewhere over the shoulder of the viewer. Perhaps he was thinking of leaving his family. On the other hand, I'm not sure if I was born when it was taken. Maybe this photograph shows the man before he had responsibilities to leave behind. It felt like it stood for something, or stood in for something: a photograph of someone that I might imagine having admired. When I looked at it I wasn't reaching for the person I knew from days in museums and visits to bookshops or the cinema. The father in the frame lived with me and I got to put him where I wanted to.

In Dundee, the last place we lived as a family, there was a green garage in the garden where Trevor painted. I remember lying on the concrete floor with paints and crayons, while he stood in front of a picture that he was working on. He was – he is – a talented artist. I told Trevor about this memory when I saw him not too long ago; I suppose I was trying to connect to the short time we lived together. He remembered it differently, that I was interrupting his work. He remembered being irritated.

In the room where I work is one of his large abstract oils. It feels like a part of a person that I barely remember knowing, he doesn't paint like that anymore. It is called 'Tree': the bare branches of a black tree are faintly visible through a constellation of oil paint droplets. Drifts of blue and orange. Enough layers of paint that it has a fractal quality, ever more complex the closer you look. Trevor's pictures have that ability to transport you. In our house I used to stare at his paintings trying to find patterns, to see what he was looking for. 'Look!' I said as a talkative four year old, 'an owl, look!' Trying to get someone's attention: 'a cat!'

At my grandfather's funeral I sat with my brother and all my cousins drinking tea and eating sandwiches. Together for the first time since we were all children. It was all surprisingly easy, my aunts wonderful, my cousins charming, the intimacy that comes from having played together as children still there to fall back on.

One of my aunts, whose house we were in, knelt on the floor as she sorted through a pile of DVDs in jewel cases. She had spent the afternoon trying to make sure everyone had the right cup of tea and the right sandwich. Now she wanted to show my brother and me the videos our grandfather had transferred to DVD. My grandfather had been a dedicated documentarian of all our childhoods, filming quietly at family occasions for decades. From my brother as a baby in our home in Norwich to us all together with our cousins and father at Christmas in Essex.

I wanted to tell her not to worry; she seemed so preoccupied and the one person who would not be in these videos was the man she was trying to grieve, my grandad. Then I realised I was being foolish: she was not trying to show me me; she was trying to show us that these videos were a line that ran between our lives and that of our grandfather. The jewel cases and the picture frames were a way for my dad's parents to hold my dad and my brother and me all together even where we had splintered off. There is a truth in photographs and in the videos, but in their ability to be rearranged in frames and on screens they conjure up relations that in reality might be more tenuous than they appear. A photograph hung on the wall of a room is just as likely to confirm absence as it is presence, and there is nothing within the frame that can tell the detective which one is the truth.

*

Pictures, and the means of displaying them, pose a threat to the landlord's walls: the things that maintain the value of their property. When renting I always felt nervous about putting things up. Nail holes, pin pricks, sticky marks left by adhesive – all these are treated as genuine threats to a property. But putting pictures on the wall is an act of making home, not because it confirms the property's physical limits but because it allows a kind of escape without admitting any threat – like a one-way-valve, an airlock.

Living in London and moving frequently meant many late nights spent trying to remove tacky blue patches or covering up holes in order to protect a deposit. There is something satisfying about putting a hole in your landlord's wall, and covering up the evidence. This tiny violence on the property is an act of recuperation. But more than this, the pictures were all pieces of other places and other people, and these connections buy a feeling of permanence; tethered to others one's life feels a little harder to shake loose from its surrounds.

Landlords and estate agents know the power of the picture frame. Framed pictures are a key part of any generic image of home. Look up an advert for a luxury apartment building, it doesn't even need to have been built. Digitally rendered homes almost always have pictures on the walls: hard to discern black and white photographs in frames, the watery blur of bad abstract expressionism, gestural squiggles with blocks of bright colour, instantly forgettable horizons, crappy Matisse-a-likes, fake Twombly vaguery. Pictures within pictures that are carefully made to provide a sense of distinction without imposing any particular taste on the scene. Cycling between flats on Rightmove, or struggling to tell the difference between photograph and CGI, you see the same paintings repeating within the algorithmic variation of identikit flat layouts.

The anthropologist Saffron Woodcraft calls the fake pictures displayed in show homes 'aesthetic traps' – little devices designed to capture a potential buyer's imagination. In the show homes Woodcraft visited near the Olympic Park in East London, she found entire fictional families assembled in silver frames placed tastefully on the furniture. These frames and families show the prospective buyer what this house might give them: a warm home inside this chilly commodity. Buy this apartment and your unborn child will graduate from university and they will love you.

Show homes bear no resemblance to specific properties; instead they are built to evoke an atmosphere for future owners to hanker after. The show home is a walk-in dream, one that you can enter into and explore fully conscious, a promise of all your wishes fulfilled. Immaculate surfaces and undisturbed furnishings, reaching out for your touch. A marketable property is one that can easily be occupied in your mind: you should be able to imagine slipping in and out with no disturbance. These generic framed images encourage the prospective buyer to imagine themselves into a property.

And so while the picture frame is a promise of permanence, it is also a sign of fungibility. You can put your picture on this wall, but so could anyone. In Bong Joon Ho's *Parasite* (2019), a working-class family exploit the neuroses of a wealthy one in order to insinuate themselves into their home. One by one, every member of the Kim family takes a job in the house of the Parks, keeping their relationship to one another secret.

When the Park house first appears, the first thing we see is a wall of framed family photographs. A professionally taken portrait of the Parks shows an apparently perfect heterosexual family arranged father beside daughter, mother beside son. They stand against a grey backdrop almost the same as the wall it is hung on. Elsewhere we see glimpses of other suitably generic artwork: large photo montages and paintings discretely integrated into the muted décor.

Even the exuberant paintings of their young son have been transformed into something else by being forced into a frame. Contained in this way, and placed side by side with other framed prints, the boy's painting cannot be play. His family views his painting as evidence of a prodigious talent, and also a disturbed nature. The leaky unconscious of the boy, which threatens to spill out into the bland interior, has to be controlled. Like the purloined letter it is disguised as something ordinary, a commodity among commodities, a trap.

The Parks' extreme wealth has bought them a place that is so perfectly tasteful as to exhibit no trace of having inhabitants at all. The Kims, on the other hand, live in a small flood-prone basement apartment at the bottom of a hill. When the wealthy Park family go on holiday the Kims move in and live in luxury. The Kims' fun is interrupted by the arrival of the former housekeeper. She is a genius of this house; she was the housekeeper of the architect who designed it. She is a part of the house, she has remained as families have come and gone.

We learn that beneath the house lies a basement where the former housekeeper's husband has been hiding from a loan shark. Until she was fired, the housekeeper had fed him on the Park family's leftovers; now he has spent days without food. Both families have established a parasitic relationship with the home. Now there is a violent stand-off between them as each threatens to reveal the other's secret, only cut short by the Parks' unexpected return. Forced to hide, the Kims find a spot underneath a coffee table where they must wait for the Parks to fall asleep before sliding silently across the polished floor on their stomachs; the frictionless interior of the home provides an escape route.

The home in *Parasite* is like a show home. It draws one family after another into its slippery domain. Who, really, is the film's 'parasite'? Is it the housekeeper and her husband, the Kim family, the Parks? Or is it the house? The building is the most sinister agent in the film. On the surface it seems inert, a pure object of exchange, but beneath the surface it harbours a secret: in the basement the bodies of the working class pile up.

Like in a dream, the images we put in picture frames are taken from our memories and wishes. But what if the connection to what is absent is illusory? Do the images we fixate upon really signify what we desire, or are we using one thing in place of another?

After a violent climax, a postscript reveals that the father of the Kim family is trapped inside the basement trying to escape the police. Upstairs the wealthy family has been replaced, a panning shot shows us the same wall with an almost identical family photograph in place. The film ends with a dream: Mr Kim's son, Ki-woo, imagines acquiring enormous wealth, enough to allow him to finally purchase the house and liberate his father from underneath it. Despite being the site of such agony, the house still serves as the frame for Ki-woo's wish fulfilment.

*

Louis Daguerre must have stared from his window out onto Boulevard du Temple hundreds and thousands of times before he was able to photograph it. Daguerre's window frame was a viewfinder long before he had worked out how to capture the light that came through it on the surface of a copper plate treated with silver halides. His photograph of the street outside his window still allows everyone with a reproduction of it to access the view from his apartment.

Daguerre developed the light-sensitive chemicals and photographic technology behind the daguerreotype, the first widely available form of photography. In 1838 he took a photograph of the Boulevard du Temple, the first photograph to capture the likeness of a living thing. The street will have been full of movement, of people rushing or strolling past, carriages taking people to work, idlers taking in the scene.

However, all this vanished in the image he made because the exposure required was so long. Only the light from two human figures created a reaction in the light-sensitive chemicals: a man standing still while having his shoes polished by a kneeling boy. The presence of the man and the shoeshine are enough to imply the full chaos of the crowd: the others are there – only vaporised. Another picture taken the same day, in which these figures do not appear, fails to capture my imagination in the same way. Daguerre did not have the technological latitude to worry about the image beyond its raw existence: a real fragment, an index of Paris.

Daguerre transformed his apartment into a camera. Safely inside, he managed the wildness of the street scenes outside by designing a method to capture the light thrown off by all those surfaces in motion. At the invention of the photograph, one of the first achievements was to take the unmanageable outside and frame it in an image that was far easier to take in.

Another photographer of near empty Parisian streets was Eugène Atget. His photographs were taken in the late nineteenth and early twentieth centuries. They are earnest and certain in their execution. For Benjamin, it was Atget who demonstrated how to 'strip away the atmosphere', the layers of performance and spectacle that were assembled in the viewfinder by those who prioritised false beauty over the shock of the world. Atget carried his heavy wooden camera around the city. It was one of those ones that concertinas like an accordion, and it still required time for images to be made: people either had to stand still or disappear.

Atget's images have a human scale. Leafing through a book of these images each one feels like I could step into it. Before he was a photographer Atget was an actor, and consciously or not he seems to reveal the city street as a stage set. Which is not to say that his images are false, but that they show the backdrop against which the action takes place. Easily ignored beneath the bustle of the crowd is a structure that underlies our experience of the city.

Benjamin thought that Atget's images had something of the crime scene about them, as if somewhere in each one was a clue: 'Isn't it the task of the photographer – descendant of the augurs and haruspices – to reveal guilt and point out the guilty in his pictures?' Augurs were Roman priests who were able to divine the future from the flight of birds, haruspices were those that could foresee events in the entrails of animals. The photograph opens up the guts of the scene for us to examine.

In one of Atget's photographs a horse shit sits on the pavement in front of L'institut de France, in another a dog waits patiently outside a door and separately, on the other side of the road, a blur of a guard stands sentry outside the Palais du Senat. At a bar called Au Petit Dunkerque the Normandy Cider was 60 centimes; a waiter leaves a ghost behind as he comes out of the door, past Atget, to serve his customers.

Photography transforms a passage of time into something both instantaneous and permanent – what alchemy! By taking something moving and making it still, the viewer gets as much time as they need to consider what the camera saw only for the length of an exposure. Atget makes it seem as if Paris in the 1890s is just waiting for a new set of actors to come onto the stage – any moment now the horse will return, the waiter will be with you presently. Daguerre's window in 1838 is still open, and if you care to you can look through it.

The messy world his camera recorded is now fixed in place; you can hold it in your hands, you can touch it on your screen. The photograph eviscerates the modern city. All that frenzied motion stilled so that we can see the only figure who can afford the luxury of waiting, the gentleman who is having his boots shined: *j'accuse!*

From my sofa I can move through one image after another, turning pages or scrolling through an image search: one instant after another, a concertina, a montage, a dream world. The photograph collapses time and space. It gives closeness even at an enormous distance. It brings your grandchildren into your living room even if you have not seen them for ten years. Minute details reach out, a twitching curtain, a handwritten price in a window display, a collar against the nape of a neck, a pigeon's flapping wings, a horse's hoof: as if one could assemble the world anew from all its bits and pieces. Like when you dream of a friend you have lost touch with and wake up so happy that you saw them, the photograph can create intimacy where there was absence.

*

> There I was alone in the apartment where she had died, looking at these pictures of my mother one by one, under the lamp gradually moving back in time with her, looking for the truth of the face that I had loved. And I found it.

Roland Barthes believed that the photograph, unlike other images, adhered to its referent; that the picture is forever attached to the real object which it represents. A photograph is always a confirmation that a thing has been within the viewfinder of a camera. After his mother died, Barthes found proof of this thesis in an image of her as a young girl. Something about that image in particular seemed true. Perhaps it was her pose that reached through time, one finger held by her other hand, the awkwardness of a child.

Barthes does not view this photograph from nowhere; he was inside her apartment when he found it and immediately placed it at the centre of his philosophy of the camera. From his mother's home he reaches out into the world, and into the past, image by image, until he finds what feels like the truth of her. The interior is the ideal place from which to venture into other places and other times. Images are secure routes away from the moment and the place of the interior, routes that can be taken without risk.

The apartment is separate from everywhere else, closed off and still. Imagine the sound of the room, the low light that requires Barthes to make use of a lamp. His mother's home is no longer animated by her presence, though perhaps there is still a dip in the upholstered couch made by years of settling down in the evening, maybe a hair clinging to an antimacassar. The house is a camera with a never-ending exposure, a record of every instant, an impossibly complex index to be interpreted by a detective, a photographer, an archaeologist, an analyst, or a haruspex. Barthes' mother, the referent, still sticks to the things around him. But it is the photograph that gives Barthes the experience of encountering her.

Barthes knows that we cannot see his mother in the photograph in the same way that he can. Nevertheless she was there to be photographed. The specificity of the photograph, according to Barthes, is its chemical relationship to the light reflected by the body of the subject.

> A sort of umbilical cord links the body of the photo-graphed thing to my gaze: light, though impalpable, is here a carnal medium, a skin I share with anyone who has been photographed.

The umbilical that Barthes describes is a real and material connection that links a photograph to its distant referent. The corporeality of photography, the certainty of the instant the shutter clicks, gives birth to an illusion: by holding a photograph we might imagine for a moment that, because the person was once out there in the world, they are still here, in the world, the photograph indicating that the 'treasury of rays' once captured by the camera continues to emanate from their body. A photograph is at once a kind of intimacy and a confirmation of absence: the subject is dead and alive, they are inside and outside of the frame.

The ambivalence of the photograph frustrates Barthes; it hints at secrets it is unwilling to give up. It is impenetrable: 'I can only sweep it with my glance, like a smooth surface.' A photo reveals a true occurrence yet refuses to tell you anything beyond what is immediately apparent. The umbilical cord reaches no further, it ends in a knot like a navel. Barthes is surely thinking of Freud's navel of the dream; the part of every dream that resists interpretation a 'knot of dream-thoughts ... that refuses to unravel'. Like dreams, photographs are proof of the existence of something that we cannot quite discern.

Picture frames and photo albums assemble pieces of life just as a dream works the residues of the day into new scenarios. On walls images are collages with hidden meaning only available to their authors. But just as with dreams, the trailing connections that recede from the image conclude in a knot. Why does this photograph feel right on the mantel? Why that postcard on the refrigerator? Each image on the wall is chosen to satisfy some desire, but it is hard to identify the wish, and even harder to understand how the image fulfils it.

Photographs are reluctant witnesses. I may know that the waiter walked out of Au Petit Dunkerque, but I do not know what drink he was carrying or who drank it. Each picture frame has the ability to infer the existence of an entire inaccessible world. On the walls of our interior they reassure us that there are other places and other times. I like to know that another world is possible, and a picture frame guarantees this possibility.

Photos in frames on mantelpieces, or in albums, or on walls are a way to pull distant people into the interior of the home. Sometimes they are our family and friends, sometimes celebrities or total strangers, and other times remote versions of ourselves. A wedding day, a first day at school, a dead relative and a tropical island that we could never afford to visit. But despite this variety, the lines of connection all lead back to a single source, like in one of those scenes in a thriller where the detective connects all the clues with pins and string. At the meeting point of these strings is a dream, your dream. You. All wishes fulfilled, and displayed within your home.

*

Gallery walls are a way of assembling a fantasy of life beyond the walls of the interior. The Wes Anderson Parisian Salon aesthetic is much loved by the generation for which a hotel is the ideal living environment. We don't know any better. In the room where I write I have two narrow shelves with an arrangement of books, postcards, and records: a studied performance of our household's cultural capital. Which is to say, I can't excuse myself from this fondness for the domestic display wall. The millennial interior is covered in frames. Art prints, vintage posters, family photos, inspirational quotes – the posters from teenage walls have been upgraded to a more sophisticated collage. With your wall of picture frames you can transform time and space, import dreams, loves, and distant places into your home, all with the minimum of work.

You can buy one ready-made: dozens of websites now offer instant gallery walls curated by influencers or tailored to your wall space and chosen aesthetic. The website Artfully Walls offers various collections promising to import a little fantasy into your dreary home, such as the 'Cottagecore Moodboard' for $361.60: 'Bring a little cottagecore into your home with this grouping celebrating the whimsy, romance and beauty of slow living in the countryside. Dream of idyllic days spent tending to the garden and rustic cozy eves in charming homes.' Or 'Floral Vision' for $780 ('Perfect for the city dweller looking to bring some greenery indoors, this gallery wall will give you your daily dose of nature').

On Desenio, the reality TV star and influencer Molly-Mae Hague's collection is made up of pale monochrome photographs, a feather, a Doric column, a woman's torso in a swimming costume. Along with these soothing images are several choice slogans: 'Create the life you can't wait to wake up to' and 'Find a way or make one'. I like the collections with slogans. I want to get a cursive font framed photo that says, 'Photographers are the descendants of augurs and haruspices' or maybe, 'All that is solid melts into air'.

Gallery walls are household shrines. They bring together dream worlds in an instant of apprehension. Your mum at your cousin's wedding, a big stone from a beach, a mindful affirmation, a geometric design, a historic map, a botanical drawing, one of those over-designed gig posters for The Arcade Fire, a picture of your feet in the surf, your dad, a vintage railway poster advertising a trip to your region, your grandmother's hands, you and your school friends on a holiday, a print of a Rothko or a Pollock, some boobs, a jolly illustration of a crowd of people dancing, a sketch of a cat made from a single line, a faux-embroidery that says 'bless this house', a still from Twin Peaks, a Lino cut of a knife and fork, you and your partner's initials in an oversized letter print style, Madonna, Maradona, Marilyn Monroe.

Molly Fischer writes about typographic posters in her essay on the millennial aesthetic. Fischer zeroes in on the slogan that best represents this specific look: 'FOR LIKE EVER' in fat sans serif capitals on top of a cloud of foam. The poster was made by designer Tracy Jenkins while she was studying for her MFA at Yale. Fischer quotes her as saying, 'I think big and dumb is valid.' After featuring on a magazine cover in 2006, the poster went viral. There are loads of things like that now, you can buy them on the Urban Outfitters website. I'm addicted to reading these phrases, they are nourishing. 'It is what it is' – smiley face shape, red text, yellow background. 'Your only limit is your soul' – multicoloured bubble letters, set against stars and a pink background. 'Be nice yeah' – all caps, hippie font, pink on green.

These phrases and images combine on the wall to create an aesthetic of meaningfulness, though even Barthes the semiologist would struggle to put his finger on precisely what that meaning is. No need to be specific; you can be certain that you are connected to... something. It is an aesthetic designed to protect you from feeling that your life is interchangeable with any other, an aesthetic that says you are uniquely hooked into the world, without making you actually confront anything or anyone. The underlying message of these affirmations is: you exist.

Some people's existence is more readily acknowledged in society than others'. Like the domestic servants in *Parasite*, some are made vulnerable so that others can feel invulnerable. Judith Butler has argued that all life shares a certain precariousness, that this shared vulnerability is what ties lives to one another. But, as Butler argues, capitalism thrives on distributing this precarity unevenly; and in the final analysis this means determining 'whose life is grievable and worth protecting and whose life is ungrievable.'

Today our right to exist is pinned to our capacity to control property. If you own your property you have a right to stay put, if you are a renter your life can be upturned at the whim of the landlord. Regardless of these conditions, a gallery wall provides a sense that you are indelibly a part of the world: how could you feel vulnerable when all of your desires and loved ones are arranged on the wall? Picture frames hold in place a set of relations that you can take down and hang somewhere else when you move. The millennial gallery wall is the aesthetic of a generation who have had to learn to be comfortable with precarious living. They are a bit of life you can pack up and take anywhere. Wherever you end up you can unpack your life and put it back together.

The search for affirmation is nothing new. The ur-domestic slogan is surely 'Live Laugh Love'. Who could disagree with its imperative? What generation has not had its moment with that particular aphorism? There are a lot of different ways to arrange these three words on your wall, in three separate frames, handwritten style, letterpress style, set against a backdrop of mountains, a metallic decal, a ceramic plate, a metal plaque.

In 1904 a woman called Bessie Anderson Stanley entered a competition in a newspaper to write an essay which defined success. She started with the line: 'He has achieved success who has lived well, laughed often, and loved much.' She won $250. However, the quote took a circuitous route into popular imagination via consistent misattribution to Ralph Waldo Emerson, ultimately being cut down to three words. It may be that the relationship advice columnist Dear Abby is responsible for bringing it into popular imagination; she attributed it to Emerson too, but eventually corrected this after a letter from Anderson Stanley's family, who are presumably not getting a cut of the profits from the millions of heart-shaped bits of wood with 'Live Laugh Love' inscribed on them.

The phrase has become a joke, the prime example of a meaningless idiom. But it deserves our attention, as all these affirmative phrases do. It is a vision of a kind of success which brings no accolades or recognition in capitalist society. To decide to live for life, love, and laughter is to dream of an escape from a society that reduces life to wealth and work. The best thing for capital to do with an idea like this, one that challenges its very basis, is to turn it into a commodity. The idiom is not a nonsense aphorism because of what it says but because you can buy it on a fridge magnet, made by alienated workers, for £2.99.

As if a purchase was ever going to allow you to escape the system which reduces you to a bank balance, a credit report, a working day, and an income.

The images and the affirmations of the gallery wall are a spell for invulnerability. We have sole power within the home to assemble the world as we wish it to be – a kind of dreamwork in service of the wish to determine one's own fate. The fantasy is that precarity is a phase we will grow out of as soon as we acquire enough capital to ensure that our lives will be properly grievable and that our children will benefit from inherited wealth.

But as with dreaming, there are deeper wishes operating below the surface. The aphoristic world of self-optimisation conceals a deeper desire for interdependency and connection. Each picture frame, like any commodity, is a social hieroglyphic, and like a photograph there is, as Barthes would say, an umbilical cord that connects the image to a web of life out there in the world. At first glance, the gallery wall appears to be born of the conviction that we can choose the lives that we are obliged to. But in the idioms repeated across these walls in living rooms across the world, and the sticky referents that hold us in relation with other people and other places, the gallery wall comes from a displaced desire to be together out in the world.

In truth we do not get to choose whom we live with, but, as Butler writes, we are 'obligated to preserve those lives and the open-ended plurality that is the global population'. Picture frames offer the promise of choosing whom we live with, but they also represent an unconscious desire to be part of something ungraspable beyond the surface of the image. They protect us against the perceived threat of precarious life, but in doing so they are a tacit reminder that what we share with everyone is vulnerability.

We have this absolute belief in the literal and figurative impermeability of our walls. The only ways in and out are windows and doors, the walls are hard, permanent, invincible – or we want them that way anyway. Privacy means being isolated, ownership means being unassailable. But then on our walls and furniture we arrange frames and images; even a postcard on a fridge is a portal to another place. They all form part of a sort of unconscious secular religion that we extend in all directions into space and time. Every image in a frame is a dream shrine, it says: you can have a better life, you are not isolated but in a web of connections.

It is easy to be snide about phrases like 'Live Laugh Love'. But this is not a statement of philosophy, it is an invocation. Like a mantra or a prayer it is a dream of pure life, pleasure, sociality, vitality unthreatened by material conditions. These are all fragments of a revolutionary dreaming; from inside our homes, and deep within ourselves, we are desperate for touch.

*

When I lived in Paris I couldn't use my phone for directions, I couldn't afford the roaming charges. So I would write directions on my hand and wrist and arm. If I felt luxurious I would print out a street map at work and fold it into my back pocket before I got on my bicycle. But mainly it was on my hands.

Sometimes I would fall asleep with my hand under my head and wake up with the names of Parisian streets reversed on my cheek, legible again when I looked in the mirror. These names would stick in my head. Rue Daguerre, maybe from a trip to the catacombs? There was a bar down there in Montparnasse that I sometimes went to with my American friends, they had befriended a French person they met in the metro and we would drink in a wine cellar that her mother owned.

In 1976 Agnès Varda released *Daguerréotypes*, a film about this street named after the pioneer photographer. While filming, she had to stay close to her home because she was caring for her young son. So she made a portrait of her street, not even the whole street, just the shops within ninety metres of her apartment – ninety metres because that's how far her power cables reached. Early in the film she films herself dressed as a nineteenth-century photographer with a wooden concertina camera. As if in a silent comedy, she attempts to arrange a portrait of a man on the street but is repeatedly interrupted by people passing by. It seems more like Atget than Daguerre – Atget the documentarian of the street, stripping off the gloss to provide an instant of truth.

Benjamin said of Atget that he 'looked for what was unremarked, forgotten, cast adrift'. The same is true of Varda; in *Daguerréotypes* she creates a portrait of her neighbourhood that has been stripped of any aesthetic sheen. She pays attention, she sits with and observes the businesses and people of her street with a care that few people afford to the places they are familiar with. We meet a husband and wife who run the local pharmacy specialising in fragrances. The couple are called the De-broussians, the woman, Marcelle, seems to have dementia. One evening, late on in the film, a mother and her daughter come in, it must be winter as they are wearing warm clothes.

The mother wants to buy some makeup for her daughter who is a little shy. Marcelle stands too close to the daughter – at one point she holds onto her coat, lifts it up and inspects it. The daughter does not react, perhaps she knows about Marcelle, but she moves closer to her mother looking awkward and embarrassed. When they leave Marcelle tries to follow them out. Her husband says, 'Don't go out' and she says, 'What, what, why?' In a voiceover we hear him explaining that every evening around 6pm she feels compelled to leave. She doesn't want to go outside but she nevertheless has an inner drive, not to leave, we are told, 'but to want to leave'. I feel overwhelmed watching this scene. She is lost in a feeling of the threshold, of wanting neither to be inside or outside. I know that feeling. We watch her look through the glass door blackened by evening, then walk out and look back in deep contemplation. Before a moment has passed, with the same resolve that she left with, she comes back in through the door.

Varda herself displays an ambivalence towards the threshold. She refuses the limit of her interior but at the same time knows she can only extend so far out into the world. The film is at once inside and outside, her cables trailing ninety metres along Rue Daguerre transmitting power to the camera that records the social life of the city while holding her to the interior where she must care for her young son.

In a crescendo in the third act of the film, Varda montages portraits of all the shops and their shopkeepers, often in poses filmed through the windows. The last question she asks everyone is, 'What do you dream about?' The shops themselves are fantastic visions, the clock repairer with a room of wallpaper and ticking carriage clocks, the bustling hairdresser, the serene cashier at the bakery sitting in the front while her husband wrestles with dough, the accordion family all arranged on chairs with accordions in hand. Each window a promise of a wish fulfilled. Varda winds her way through the high street, her portraits, her daguerreotypes drawing together this cosmos in thousands of frames.

Her referents are all bound together by the web she traces around her home. The critic So Mayer talks about how Varda reflected on the film later in her career:

> Using the word 'cord,' she suggests it's also an umbilical connection between her own family community, and the street beyond that will, implicitly, help raise her children just as she helped to document and preserve the unique community in which she – l'auteure de quartier – made her work.

Varda is collapsing the boundary between her house and the world. Her portraits in *Daguerréotypes* are a conscious realisation of the dreaming that takes place when we arrange frames on the walls of our homes. Varda knows that her home is always a part of her street, and that the bourgeois fantasy of isolation is only surface: her cables materialise the umbilical cords that link together inside and outside. Varda's life in her apartment cannot be reasonably separated from the people who live on her street. She shares in their precarious lives.

In another, much later film, *Les Glaneurs et la Glaneuse*, Varda shows us another way the world outside creeps into the interior. Varda films water stains left behind in the white paint on her ceiling, the water is coming in through a hole in the roof that she hasn't had repaired. The stain is golden brown and it spreads like a web, or a flower, or a mushroom. She makes three close-ups of different parts of the ceiling, each set in a gaudy golden frame with the name of an artist whose work she thinks the stain resembles. As in *Daguerréotypes*, her home is porous; she does not seal it off but meets the water's ingress with her gaze. Framing this leak as a work of art, Varda reminds us that the images we frame and mount on our walls are also fissures through which other worlds, other places, and other times can make their way into our homes.

*

The picture frame is a way to protect ourselves from the world outside by selecting only the lives we want to let in. But each image may yet still be punctured by lives we do not know. Like the shoe-shine boy in Daguerre's photograph, dead now, impossible to identify, but still somehow alive in the index of reflected rays that once came through the window of Daguerre's apartment. No picture can be entirely contained by its frame. We do not get to define the boundaries of our life.

In 2001 my father made a small painting for his parents. It shows a beach filled with sea lavender as far as far as the eye can see. The plants seem to stretch beyond even the grey horizon above the stony coastal landscape. Sea lavender plants reproduce themselves sometimes by seed and sometimes by rhizome – root tendrils sent out by one plant to clone themselves into another, and another, and another. Along the east coast of England, sea lavender faces inundation by seawater one minute and by freshwater the next. Yet it thrives in the fluctuating salinity of a coastline where generations of my father's family have travelled, walked, and worked the land.

Living on through cycles of dominance and die-back, sea lavender is one of those plants that can make difficult landscapes feel so full of life. The vulnerability of life is also the source of its abundance, as Anna Lowenhaupt Tsing puts it: 'Indeterminacy, the unplanned nature of time, is frightening, but thinking through precarity makes it evident that indeterminacy also makes life possible.' All the pictures and photos held together on the wall of my dad's parents' home, and the handful which are now out of their Sainsbury's bag for life and spread out on the bed in the room where I am writing.

I live in Essex now and I walk sea walls overlooking marshes full of sea lavender. I look at distant birds knowing that my father and his parents would know all their names. Maybe I should hang these pictures on my wall together with the large oil painting by my dad. Knotting together into a dream montage all the ways, known and unknown to me, that I am tied into the life outside my house; even when some of those links do not sit easy with me.

HOUSE PLANTS

Tender geraniums come in and out of Galvey through the big bay window in the room my mother's parents call the green room. I watched television in there, kneeling or sitting or lying on the moth-eaten yellow carpet while eating fried egg sandwiches made for me by my grandfather, who we call Grumpy. He would hang in the doorway and watch *Sesame Street* with me. He pretended he was checking in but really he liked to watch the programme too, particularly Oscar the Grouch.

The smell of geraniums is powdery and floral but also, somehow, astringent. They lived on a green cast iron stand, two staggered shelves for the pots to sit on. One year Grumpy cut out the cats from the front of some cat food boxes and stuck them to sticks before standing them up in the soil to stop the cats pissing on the plants. He was trying out on the cats the same wind-up he'd used on us when he cut out the picture from the front of a packet of Carr's Water Biscuits and served them to me and my brother on a plate.

I would get as close to the television as I could. My sandwich squeezed in my small hands would drip egg yolk onto the carpet. There was an armchair that was so old that it was uncomfortable to sit on in almost every place, its arms were upholstered around an iron frame which was slowly breaking through, it was stuffed with horsehair and you could hear the springs when you sat on it. The chair was covered in William Morris fabric, green with plants wending across it. I liked it in the winter when the geraniums were inside and it got dark early enough that I was allowed to play in the garden with a flashlight. I always wanted to be allowed to climb in and out of the windows and, when unwatched, this is exactly what I did.

Geraniums are the common name for *pelargoniums* although, confusingly, there is an entirely separate genus also called *geranium*. Like so many of the most familiar features of British homes they come from another part of the world. They are native to South Africa and first appeared in a botanical garden in Leiden around 1600. In 1631 the English gardener and botanist John Tradescant bought pelargonium seeds from a merchant in Paris and planted them in his garden in Kent.

The plant was probably collected by mariners who had stopped at the Cape of Good Hope for rest and replenishment while sailing between Europe and Asia. It may have even been traded with the Khoe or !Ui-speaking nomadic peoples who lived in Southern Africa before being driven out by Dutch settlers.

The first permanent settlement was established in 1652. When nomadic first nations people arrived to find the Dutch where they would usually expect to graze cattle, they repeatedly raided the settlers, stealing cattle and otherwise expressing their disregard for the people who thought they had a right to make themselves a permanent feature of the landscape. Through a combination of war and disease, the Dutch ultimately put an end to the resistance of these peoples with the brutality that characterised European colonisation.

Empires frequently used the smokescreen of scientific knowledge to reinforce their right to claim land that was not theirs. European colonists went out into the world with the utter confidence that they, and only they, were capable of understanding it. This understanding underpinned what they felt was a right to dominate. The use of triangulation to measure distances in map-making was first undertaken by the British in India. The ancient cultures of the world were pillaged – 'deciphered' – by enthusiastic racists, and plants, animals, and humans were all figured into rigid taxa.

Modern botany emerged in parallel with Empire because plants, and the movement of plants around the world, were among the primary ways that imperial powers were able to generate profit. By understanding which plants grew where and under what conditions, it became possible for flora to be taken from one place and transported to colonies where ideal climates existed for their cultivation. It was the science of botany that enabled cotton to be grown in the Americas, sugarcane in the Caribbean. These agricultural innovations were often only profitable because of the labour of enslaved Africans, and the success of such industries drove the demand for the trade in enslaved people. Botany is entangled with the fallacious race science that was deployed to justify slavery, and the maritime engineering which conspired to transport African bodies.

The transportation and science of plant life developed in parallel to the transportation and pseudoscience of human life. Linnaeus, in addition to establishing the science of botanical taxonomy, also proposed a hierarchy of human life according to skin colour. Maritime engineers conspired to maximise the number of people that could be transformed into cargo in ever more person-destroying arrangements. The suffering and resistance of enslaved people was treated as a logistical problem, just as it was for the transportation of flora.

The significant challenge for plant collectors was how to move live plants around the world. Up until now, most plants had been transported as seeds, rhizomes, or dried specimens. Then in 1833, the same year that Britain passed a law to outlaw slavery, Nathaniel Ward successfully shipped British ferns to Australia in a glass box which would be later known as a 'Wardian case'. Now instead of transporting people the British could transport plants to places where they could violently exploit human labour by other means.

The ancestor of the modern terrarium, the Wardian case was a sealed glass enclosure that protected plants from salt spray on ship decks while still allowing them sunlight. The enclosed atmosphere also ensured that the plants needed minimal care during the trip since moisture could circulate in the glazed habitats, a kind of miniature landscape. Like the nineteenth-century interior, the Wardian case both trapped its inhabitants and protected them from the forces of the outside world.

The Wardian case created a revolution in the transportation of plants. Not only did it bring ornamental specimens to botanical collections and homes around the world, it also allowed the British to smuggle tea plants from China to establish plantations in India. But Wardian cases were not only used to transport plants; in the bourgeois interior of the nineteenth century, they were also used to display them. Long before the terrariums of the millennial interior there was the fashion for Wardian cases filled with ferns, creating a craze for the plants known as 'Pteridomania'. Ferns, with their tolerance for humidity, low light, and intermittent rain, fitted perfectly with the orientalist fantasy of the bourgeois home. This craze provoked a game of acquisitive exploration at the domestic scale: popular books on fern taxonomy, weekend trips to the countryside with the hope of 'discovering' new species – all the trappings of glamorous colonial exploration made available to the curious middle classes.

Pteridomania was not limited to the plants themselves; it also influenced decorative trends in ironwork, ceramics, and textiles. The pattern commonly printed on the custard cream biscuit is derived from this decorative craze. The limited number of domestic varieties led to ferns being imported from across the Empire. Obsessive collectors sought out ever-rarer varieties to display in their living rooms.

Just as it enabled the transportation of plants internationally, in the home the Wardian case enabled plants to survive in the modern environment. Within the living rooms of British cities they protected woodland ferns from polluted air and maintained their favoured damp atmosphere. The Wardian case was a machine for turning plants into commodities, and thanks to these hermetically sealed cases, the colonial impulse to collect and taxonomise was transformed into a parlour game.

The first house plants flourished despite the hostile atmosphere of the bourgeois home. Chief among these was the so-called 'cast-iron plant' or aspidistra, native to China and Vietnam. The aspidistra's ability to defy the odds is lauded in an 1894 book, *Greenhouse and Stove Plants*:

> Aspidistras have the merit of thriving under conditions of deficient light and a dry atmosphere, such as few plants can endure at all. Hence they are amongst the best room plants for growing in towns, not simply existing, but growing in a way that bids defiance to adverse surroundings.

The nineteenth-century city dweller had learned to accept that the interior was lethal to all but the most enduring of flora. By the end of the century, the aspidistra had become ubiquitous in the living rooms of the Victorian metropolis. Yet the plant remained mysterious: for as long as a century some scientists continued to believe that their creepy soil-level flowers were pollinated by snails and slugs, a process called malacophily.

Like many of the trappings of the Victorian British home, the aspidistra was adopted from the glamorous interiors of Paris. An 1868 book called *Gleanings from French Gardens* introduced the aspidistra to British audiences, stating that the plants have 'a very important place in the decoration of apartments'. This was not a cheap plant, and when it began to appear in catalogues in the 1860s, William Bull's nursery in Chelsea charged more than ten shillings, equivalent to two days' wages for a skilled worker.

In the nineteenth century a single aspidistra had the ability to distinguish a bourgeois home. The aspidistra was a symbol of sophistication and respectability, hence its common inclusion in photographic portraiture. And like a picture frame it was a way to display a worldly connection: a portal to an imagined Oriental boudoir or at least a chic Parisian parlour. However, by the twentieth century the glamour of the aspidistra had faded. Though they were still common, aspidistras, like chintz, had become a signifier of fusty domesticity. Everyone had one somewhere, gathering dust.

George Orwell's disdain for the tenacious values of Victorian respectability among the middle class of 1930s Britain is the central theme of his book *Keep the Aspidistra Flying* (1936). Its protagonist Gordon Comstock decides to reject the vulgar decency of a career in advertising in order to focus on his poetry. He takes a cheap room in a 'dingy and depressing' part of northwest London where he begins a 'secret feud' with the aspidistra in his room. The house of his landlady Mrs Wisbeach is full of aspidistras, and even as he tries to remove himself from society he finds himself smothered by the way its oppressive values are embodied in the interior. For Orwell the aspidistra symbolised the lethargic conservatism of English society: 'It ought to be on our coat of arms instead of the lion and the unicorn. There will be no revolution in England while there are aspidistras in the windows.'

Orwell seems to be borrowing from a surreal short story by W. F. Harvey, 'The Man Who Hated Aspidistras'. In Harvey's story Ferdinand, a writer and literary scholar, who, as a child, acquired the habit of tormenting and torturing aspidistras in his aunt's house, is himself ultimately reduced to the status of an aspidistra in a seeming act of revenge. Ferdinand's writing style and his wits dull until, now living in the house he has inherited from his aunt, all he can do is sit in a corner and wait for the occasions when he is wheeled outside by a servant so that he can soak up the rain.

In Orwell's novel the vegetative state Comstock is reduced to is less literal. In a cruel and peculiar ending, Comstock returns home to a respectable life. Having returned to advertising, we are told, he now writes better than ever, composing copy for an advertising campaign for a treatment for sweaty feet ('pedic perspiration'). Reunited with his wife, he moves into a flat in Edgware. All is not rosy as they row about whether or not to buy an aspidistra, but he persuades her to do so, and as they leave the house to acquire one she feels a kick from the baby that they are having together. Are we to feel sorry for this man trapped in his own banal nightmare? Or are we to believe that he has truly found happiness? It could be read as a lowkey precursor to *1984*: like the aspidistra, Comstock has found a satisfying life inside a container, but Orwell asks us – what kind of a life is it?

The life of the houseplant, however reduced, is still life. In her 1938 song 'The Biggest Aspidistra in the World', the actor and musician Gracie Fields zeroes in on something revolutionary about the familiar household plant in its capacity to exceed the limits placed on it.

Fields, affectionately known as Our Gracie, was born in 1898, and grew up above a chip shop in Rochdale. She started acting as a child on the local music hall circuit before becoming a West End and Hollywood star. 'The Biggest Aspidistra in the World' is a fairy-tale of working class triumph, a sardonic narrative of the most banal thing imaginable becoming remarkable: 'For years we had an aspidistra in a flowerpot, / On the whatnot, near the 'atstand in the 'all'. The singer's brother has decided to cross the sad looking aspidistra with an oak tree and plant it outside, and at this point 'it shot up like a rocket. 'Til it's nearly reached the sky'. The house plant, which had long ceased to impress the neighbours, now towers over the neighbourhood, and it gets so large that it begins to overtake the area surrounding their home: 'The roots stuff up the drains, grow along the country lanes, / And they came up half a mile outside the town'.

The joy of this song, among Fields' most famous, is that this icon of domestic tedium is made extraordinary. The aspidistra destroys the tiresome boundaries of the home. In contrast to the pseudo-insurrection of Ikea's 'chuck out the chintz' advert, this song opens up something genuinely radical. Like Gracie Fields, herself a master code-switcher, the aspidistra of the song explodes the limits of both class and the interior. The biggest aspidistra in the world is a revolutionary hymn. It is a call to let life escape the boundaries of property, to explode the walls that separate inside and out. Where Orwell saw the plant as a signifier of defeat, Fields saw the potential for victory.

Like Walter Benjamin, Fields has uncovered the secret inside the commodity: the everyday objects we use to decorate our homes are filled with life. Once we recognise the social nature of these objects, that they are the product of the labour of other people in other places, and that we own them only at the expense of those exploited workers, then – well – all that is solid melts into air.

*

At Galvey the best house plants are the ones that grow through the windows, and sometimes the walls. The outside has always been welcome inside my grandparents' home. A tendril of ivy or a bramble often found its way through the windows or straight through the wooden walls.

Undeniably it is a luxury of wealth that they can show such disregard for the future value of their property; but there is also an ethics to their negligence. Today my grandmother spends a lot of time sitting by the sliding glass doors looking at their wild and beautiful garden, deer and birds wandering in and out of frame. With my Aunt Hannah she made a map of the territories of all of the birds: the trees they prefer, the windfall apples they defend. My grandmother has inverted the Wardian case. From within her house she can watch the life outdoors. The curious plants reaching in, or the deer that come close to the window to observe her, are reminders that the inside is always also outside. My grandmother has always been uncomfortable with the imperative to dominate the landscape. Before she became ill I stood next to her doing the washing up while looking out the window at a rat cleaning itself on the bird bath, and she said, 'I know that I am supposed to want it dead, but it is so beautiful.'

In an essay about being an only child, my grandmother once wrote:

> Across the gravel drive there was an abandoned field of shrubs and stunted trees that had been completely overgrown by honeysuckle. I could crawl inside one particular dim, sweet-scented room that was entirely mine. I found some flat fungi growing out of a tree trunk that were large enough to make imaginary plates, but no guests ever came, nor, to be honest, did I want them to.

What is wonderful about these dinner plates, as with Fields's aspidistra, is the indeterminacy and excess of the non-human. Outside the geometric logic of rooms and walls, we may catch a glimpse of a different kind of life, one where we live *with* and not in spite of the other lives that we depend on. There is something uncanny about the house plant. Somewhere between furniture and inhabitant, they require the barest nourishment, and yet they persist! Were they to regularly escape their pots, climb walls, burrow through plaster, and lift floorboards, then they would surely be deemed a menace. But they are tolerated because of their relative obedience, an essential quality for a possession.

The house plant is a way to let in a little piece of beguiling non-human life without it threatening to undermine the foundations. But you should know that given half a chance they would take over the whole place. Perhaps this is why we like them – because we share with them

an instinctual drive to escape the limits of our containers. 'The Biggest Aspidistra in the World' suggests that the
house plant dreams of escaping the home and stuffing up
the drains. Where Orwell's aspidistra symbolises a sort
of death-by-respectability, the house plant knows that it
stands for the opposite.

Galvey is a bungalow made from a kit bought from Colt
Houses. It was built in the sixties by my grandmother's
aunts Doris and Marjorie. When my grandparents moved
there from London in the late eighties they added a
church hall from the Colt Houses catalogue. This is where
my grandfather paints. When I phoned him recently to
ask him about his geraniums, he said, 'I'm painting but I
can hold the phone with this hand,' and then, after a brief
chat, 'The light is going so you have to stop now.'

The house is porous, it does not do very well at keeping the outside out. Its frame is wooden, the roof and
walls are clad in cedar shingles and require frequent re-
pair. In my teens, I spent my summers listening to the ra-
dio on the roof, stripping rotten tiles and replacing them
with new ones. I was paid a flat rate per shingle. They
smelled of turpentine, the shingles, just like the inside of
the house where you are still liable to get oil paint on you
if you are not careful. When this happens my grandfather
will chase you through the house with a turpentine
soaked rag to clean off the paint.

There was a special tool for the roof, a long flat piece
of metal which ended in a thin and flexible arrowhead
shape. You slipped it under the shingles to try to break
through the nails and lift them away from the battens.

My mum, Emily, told me that she fell off the roof while helping build the studio, and that we would be able to find her chewing gum stuck beneath shingles up there.

It was always very satisfying when a large number of tiles came away at once, though when you came across stubborn nails you had to use pliers to remove them one at a time. Once or twice I opened up the roof to find an empty wasp nest to admire; one year my brother found one that was still occupied and got out of roof-mending for the summer. There was no roof felt and in places you could see right down into the attic as you worked. At lunch we would eat cheese and salad and my grandmother would empty the salad bowl onto her plate and mop up the dressing with bread.

My grandfather did not believe in building walls for us. He told my brother and me that any kind of rail or wall around our treehouses would make us more likely to fall because we would not be careful enough. So we had two platforms in trees in the front garden. These treehouses were the shakiest of edifices: planks nailed together to make a platform with nothing to keep us from the edge. I loved climbing ladders and each had a different quality: the tall metal one, a shorter wooden stepladder, or the beautiful red wooden ladder with several rotten rungs reinforced with bits of two-by-four. From the trees in the winter I could see the house, the neighbours and the pub over the road. In the summer it was as if I was entering my own green room, with real-life William Morris wallpaper as decoration. Like my grandmother's mushroom-filled hideaway, the treehouses were an experiment in privacy; when I was up there the trees in the garden were mine.

Being able to be alone as a child was among my many privileges. Occasionally I bargained for the right to eat a meal in a tree; these moments felt like such utter triumph, a taste of what adulthood would surely feel like.

The imaginative world of children is full of plant life. The first film I ever saw in the cinema was *The Secret Garden* (1993), Agnieszka Holland's adaptation of the 1911 novel by Francis Hodgson Burnett. Mary Lennox has been sent to live in her uncle's home in Yorkshire after her parents' death in colonised India, and here she finds herself in a large and miserable interior. Her uncle is a grim pre-Raphaelite-alike widower. One of her few dealings with the man is her going into his study to ask him for 'a bit of earth', all she thinks she needs to survive in this strange new place. After agreeing to her request he finds himself overwhelmed by his own feelings, and he immediately goes into exile.

While wandering the grounds Mary finds a walled area that is locked behind a door. She meets Dickon, an enigmatic working-class boy who is always outdoors. Together they bring the garden back to life; with plants, they revive the creaking and miserable grounds outside the house. At night she hears crying, and eventually she finds Colin, her pale and ghostly cousin who has been permanently infantilised by the fawning treatment he receives from doctors and servants. Mary bullies Colin until he comes outdoors, at which point everyone is astounded that he does not immediately die. Revived by the world outside, Colin learns what it is to play and to live outside of his container, and with Mary's encouragement he makes a wish for his father's return.

Ultimately the family and the house, long haunted by the death of Colin's mother, are revived by the now blooming garden, and by moving their lives back out into the world. The life inside the walled garden bursts out. The father's return takes place while the children are playing blind man's bluff among wildflowers, gothic follies, and cascading lilacs. The father sees his son as if for the first time; where once everything seemed moribund, now he can acknowledge that his son is alive.

In my childhood imagination this is what could happen in the garden. In secret dens children could take over the world. With your own bit of earth you could remake the world: your father could return, you and your friends could play forever, you would be in charge. Children see what adults often ignore, the revolutionary potential of the life outside the interior, where there is so much space, so much generative potential, that surely we can each find a life of utmost pleasure. It is as if children have an intuition for the ability of life to always break free of the containers that adults seem determined to place around it.

As a child I hated *E.T.* (1982). We had it recorded on a VHS tape that my younger brother liked to watch again and again and again. But it scared me. Not the alien, the men – especially once E.T. has been discovered and the sinister forces of US state power break into the suburban household of Elliott and his siblings, and poor E.T. is experimented on until he almost dies.

E.T. starts with utopia: the alien who eats hummus and watches cartoons transforms a young boy's understanding of the world. Somehow their bodies and spirits

become entangled. Suddenly everything is possible. Elliott starts a revolution, freeing frogs from glass jars in
the middle of a biology classroom. With frogs all over the
floor Elliott climbs onto the back of a larger boy so that
he can kiss the girl with blond hair and patent leather
shoes before escaping out into the world along with all
the frogs. Like *The Secret Garden*, *E.T.* is a dream of utter transformation. The limits that we place around life
are made by adults, as the promise for everything alive to
grow beyond its limits conflicts with the logic of adulthood and modernity.

Early in the film Elliott's sister Gertie brings E.T. a
plant pot containing some dead dahlias. E.T. demonstrates his power by reviving the flowers, but once the
adult world has broken in and begun its experiments on
the extra terrestrial his life begins to falter, and the dahlias begin to die. E.T. cannot survive inside the limits that
society seeks to put around him.

In the dream interior of my childhood dens it felt as if
I could simply make a place for myself to live wherever I
felt like it. Today that dream remains only in the muted
wilderness of the pot plants in my study. The pot plant
can go with you wherever you go. It is a mobile form of
life that we can prevent from extending its roots beyond
its container. It doesn't need a permanent habitat, you can
move it from home to home. The house plant thrives in
precarity, just as we are expected to. All it needs is a little
earth, some plant food, and it too can persist. Isn't this so
much less than what we were promised?

*

Fig trees are interesting – sort of kinky – in that they produce more fruit when their roots are contained. One afternoon when I was a teenager I dug a hole outside my mum's back door deep enough to sink an entire plastic bin into, inside of which we planted a fig tree intended to annoy my grandfather by producing more and better figs than his tree.

The fig tree at Galvey – probably spurred on by the climate crisis – has recently begun to produce a bonanza every year. Maybe the house itself is providing the resistance that the tree needs to produce. Roots and foundations competing for space and, up above, bursting purple fruit ripen and drop before bouncing off the roof and falling on the ground for wasps and birds to eat.

As Anna Lowenhaupt Tsing has suggested, when one kind of life comes up against another the indeterminacy can be frightening, but it can also be generative. On a holiday in Rome I saw fig trees grow like weeds. Huge ungainly plants lean over the Tiber; below, where fruit have rolled and seeds have been deposited by animal droppings, saplings reach up from the banks all thin and supple, their leaves like hands. All the while their roots undermine the concrete that holds the river in place. Near Gramsci's grave in the Protestant cemetery a fig tree grows out of the trunk of a conifer tree.

The prevailing logic is that we cannot allow anything to damage the places we live in. We must stave off decay, and at the same time prevent growth. The interior is a commodity and so we must protect it from life. But neither plants nor humans can truly inhabit the spaces they live in unless they are also allowed to transform them.

The artist Rachel Adams spent the pandemic making immaculate mushrooms and attaching them to the pages of every issue of *Elle Decoration* that she received in the post. Seeing pages of fantasy interiors promote such fungal growth reveals a vision of vegetal insurrection. The dead commodity of the interior being undone by a form of life associated with decay.

Aspidistras share an interspecies kinship with mushrooms. Their icky globular ground-level flowers are thought to mimic fungi to draw the attention of the gnats and hopping land crustaceans that pollinate them. As a child, my grandmother knew that mushrooms were a kind of forest crockery and, indeed, the name 'toadstools' imagines mushrooms as a seat for slimy croaking amphibians. Unlike the home, plants constantly change and shape new habitats for animals and children alike. I wonder what might happen if we let houseplants truly bring the interior to life? Might our desire to abide with these uncanniest of lifeforms inspire us to reformulate the interior as habitat instead of commodity?

*

My grandmother likes to grow things from the discarded seeds and pits of fruit. She experiments with the occasional avocado stone suspended above a dish of water with cocktail sticks, and her attempts to sprout lemon seeds and apple pips are now a dedicated operation.

Seven or eight years ago she had a stroke after a fall. She could speak but little she said related to the world around her. Once she told me as I left, 'Let's communi-

cate via scented lavender water.' When she was first unwell there was a long-running narrative about her desire
to establish something called 'animal forensics', though
it seemed to vary as to whether this crime fighting force
was designed to protect animals from humans or vice ver-
sa. She is a writer, and a doctor suggested that her imagination and ability to tell stories were filling in where she
could not otherwise find the words to speak. She cannot
walk, but though she gets tired easily she can once again
tell stories. When she first started to write again she sat in
the garden with her notebook and wrote letter after letter
but all on top of one another, until doctors, her carer, and
her children helped her begin to move across the page.

Access to the garden is all important at Galvey, and
every time I visit there is an adaptation to the route out
from the green room and into the garden through the
large aluminium sliding doors. A constant programme
of adjustments to the decking and repairs to a ramp are
made to ensure that Grumpy can move my grandmother.
They cannot bear to be separated from the outdoors, even
as it works its way into their home. Last year on the way
into the garden he slipped and she was tipped out of her
chair; Grumpy badly hurt his shoulder. But they will not
give up their time together outside: drinking coffee and
eating biscuits while my grandmother decides on a new
plan for a pond, a greenhouse, or a plant.

I cannot imagine the two of them dying. They are constantly talking to each other, exchanging ideas, bickering,
planning. Like the ivy growing into the house, they have
a strong foothold in the landscape. For them, as it was for
me as a child, the house has never been a set of limits but

instead each room and each part of the garden offers a new habitat, and an opportunity to play.

The house is alive, and every adjustment they make seems to be a joy to them; they are living together. This is undeniably a privilege, but it is one that I know that they would wish could be afforded to everyone. Sometimes when I go home you can tell that they think they are about to die. My grandfather in particular is prone to this sort of mood. You know because he gives you money and he shakes your hand, as if this is what he always does. Everything there is so alive, I don't know why I worry about them dying, because I am certain that they will always be alive and living in Galvey.

When he was a little boy, my grandfather was given a gnome-shaped candle for Christmas. It was still light outside but he wanted to see how it would illuminate the dark. He tried it all over the house until he closed the curtains of his sister's bedroom and climbed under the bed. This was the best place to see how well the flame on top of the little gnome's head would glow. Then he went downstairs to sing to his mother. Then he went outside to play. And soon enough the candle had set a fire which burned up the whole bed. This, unfortunately, is all I get of the story because my mum says he is watching an episode of *Perry Mason* now.

Between the first draft and the final draft of this chapter Galvey burned down. One Saturday morning the house caught fire, its old dry timber welcomed its doom and flames ripped through the household in no time at all. With good fortune my grandmother was being visited by her physiotherapist who was able to carry her out and prevent Grumpy going back in to get more things. Both of my grandparents and their wonderful carer made it out. Now they live in an apartment close to my mother where they look out on the river. If you take the shortcut to the train station you'll see them trying to follow the plot of a detective programme, my grandmother's sleeping face illuminated by *Endeavour.*

They are rebuilding. This time the house will be more accessible to wheelchairs and less vulnerable to fire. The two of them are determined. They did not pause for breath; my grandfather is drawing every day, trying to make up for the drawings that he lost in the fire, while my grandmother recently published a book about the gardens at Rousham, in Oxfordshire, with the publisher that they made for themselves. It was Grumpy's idea to call it Academy Press which he feels gives it the requisite gravitas. You can't buy one but you may find one in the library, or if you ask my grandparents they may still have a copy.

A few weeks ago, I unlocked the padlock and shifted the fence that was there to secure the site and walked into the drive with Rebecca. I had spent a week playing my reaction through my mind in advance. Would my knees weaken. Would I remain stoic and calm.

It was hard to take in, the burned carcass, the carbonised home. It was alien and impossible to understand. I bent over like a detective near where my bedroom window used to be and picked up a packet of photographs, all fused together and singed. I peeled them apart and there were me and my brother asleep as children, there we were eating lunch outside in Essex with our cousins.

I stood in the green room, or where the green room had been. In front of me was the chimney and the hearth, the bricks left exposed as everything else was burned away. It was hard to bring to mind the egg sandwiches and pelargoniums. The house wasn't alive. In my grandmother's study were some of the burned books. Her father's books, her own books, the box file that said MONSTERS. The room where she would be sleeping when it was time to sit down and eat. And the piano where Grumps used to sit and play 'Lady Be Good' when he was supposed to be doing something useful. It was just wires and bolts all mixed in with the ashes of sheet music.

But outside the garden is alive. I sit on the swing made with long blue rope hanging from a branch which has thickened enough that it still holds my weight, maybe thirty years since it was first asked to. I walk it back as far as I can and push myself off. My feet straight in front of me and my head back I look around me at the plants and trees and flowers still doing everything they can.

My grandmother said to me, 'The wonderful thing is, we still have the garden, and we can go up there and grow things,' and Grumpy is trying to get the architect to remove the fig tree from the plans so that no one tells him it has to be taken down. Aside from some curled leaves and blackened boughs the tree survived. The garden is waiting for them to come home and, in front of the house, down near the charred surface of a flower bed by the front door, little purple hands reach upwards.

BLANKETS

Picture me as a small child. I am pushing the point of a pencil hard against the surface of the paper so that I can eke out a line with certainty. I am drawing a bird, it has a huge beak and large feet. It has two legs, one longer than the other, and feet with five toes each that explode from the ankle like a firework. Now here I am on another day. Now my task is to draw a lizard. It is pictured from the side: two legs, one eye and a tail that sticks right out hovering just above the ground. It is a tidy fellow, a stern companion to the exuberant bird.

I cannot summon any memory of making these two animals, but how they must have lived for me in the moment as I summoned them into the paper plane! Now I am writing with them draped over my legs, each one appliquéd dozens of times in different patterned fabrics across the surface of a large quilt made for me by my mum, Emily. One piece is yellow with small red polka dots, the material that she used to make my brother and me a pair of stuffed dinosaurs when we were children. The centre of the quilt is a yellow sun and radiating out from that point are stitched concentric circles interrupted by smaller rounds of stitching. It has the geometry of a solar system.

Em began making the quilt soon after I drew the pictures but for much of my life the centre part of this quilt top was folded up in a bag alongside the paper templates for the animals and a number of patches already cut out. Sometimes I would find it when I was nosing through the things in her study, hoping for a treat, a Christmas present.

I had thought it a gesture abandoned, my dream animals forgotten. The stitching is the Penelope work of concentration. What Em calls 'tiny mouse's stitches' running rings around the material. The stitches attach the quilt top to a piece of block-printed chintz. Sandwiched between is a layer of wadding which gives the quilt surface an undulating effect as it is compressed by stitches in some places and allowed to expand in others. I did not know that she had returned to the task. When she did her hands and eyes could not manage the impossibly fastidious hand-stitching that began the project. The final bits of quilting, more circles and now spirals also, were added by machine.

It was my Christmas present the year that Rebecca and I got married. I felt a plummeting feeling when I unwrapped it. Its existence left me unsteady and I sobbed. It was the freight of decades, and the hours of work made it feel like an impossible object. Like Proust's mother coming up after he had been sent to bed, this was a childhood wish fulfilled.

The quilt appeared from nowhere, like an embrace that I had once wanted but had now forgotten – here was something I did not know I yearned for. It spanned nearly my entire life and it means everything to me. It connects everything with everything. Like the stitches which work like wormholes joining together each layer of material – each one a cosmos. This quilt is not only an object that holds me like a parent; it holds me like the world does.

When I was small I stayed up late worrying about the thoughts that other people were having, ones I could not know. Everybody I met, could I be certain that they thought as I did? What could I know of their lives? It horrified me. As a boy I dreamed about being on a spaceship invaded by aliens, all my crew mates dead, my boiler suit promising no protection, the airlocks open, the breath taken from my lungs. Alienated from everything, my lungs emptied by the vacuum. The quilt is like the reassurance I used to get from knowing Em was next door watching *Morse* with my grandparents, that they existed at least. Against the threat of disappearing in the night, just disintegrating because everyone has forgotten me, is the quilt. It is as if she has tucked me in. Held in place by blankets, I know I will still be there in the morning.

Blankets hold you without a person there to hold you. Particularly useful while your consciousness unravels into the frayed work of remembering and forgetting; of dreaming. And while most blankets are made by people you do not know, they are there for you nonetheless.

*

In a bath in a three-storey house in Herne Hill I tried my best to translate the German poetry that Rebecca was reading me from her perch on the toilet: 'Ich bin nicht tot nicht ganz: ich bin / Schrödinger's Katz.' Something like, 'I am not dead not fully: I am / Schrödinger's cat.'

We had been together six months. Rebecca had taken an austere room in a house in South London, then quickly realised she was a lodger in someone else's breakdown. The house was too big, it was full of half painted walls, dying plants, and abandoned craft projects, a son we heard but did not see.

Hiding in the bathroom together we were talking about Penelope, Odysseus' wife and queen of Ithaca. The line from the poem is in Penelope's voice. It comes from Barbara Koehler's *Niemands Frau,* a feminist rewriting of Homer's epic. Koehler presented her poem as a kind of tapestry, weaving countless names and strands of thought through the source text: quantum physics, Derek Jarman, Alan Turing, Wittgenstein, and many others. When she read aloud she would weave in the air with one hand as she spoke.

When Odysseus did not come home from the Trojan War, Penelope was left to maintain a household and a family. She raised her young son while being assailed by suitors who camped out in her home, each one trying to persuade her that her husband was dead and that he was the man for her. She diverted the suitors with a ruse playing on men's ignorance of weaving, telling them that she would make her decision once she had finished making the death shroud for Odysseus' father Laertes. All day she sat at her loom making steady progress, and every night she would undo her work only to start again the following morning. Hidden from view like Schrödinger's

Cat, the weaving was in a state of quantum oscillation between being and not-being. She preserved herself by creating a state of indeterminacy to shelter in.

Penelope seizes a part of space and time to command for herself. In her monograph on Koehler's poem, Rebecca writes that, through her weaving, 'Penelope guards the plural potential of her own space and time.' This is the magic of the woven; it links things together, it holds things in tension, it defines a length and a breadth and a depth, and, in doing so, it has the capacity to define its own particular space and time. In his essay 'The Image of Proust', Walter Benjamin reminds us that the word *text*, like *textile*, is derived from the Latin word for web: *textum*. Reading against the grain, Benjamin argues that Proust's great novel is just as much about forgetfulness as it is remembering, calling it 'a Penelope work of forgetting' in which 'remembrance is the woof and forgetting is the warf'.

Towards the end of his life, trying finish his work, Proust confined himself to his sparsely furnished Parisian apartment, sequestering himself away like Penelope or Schrödinger's cat. He lined the walls with cork in order to keep the outside world out while he wove his text. In his essay, Benjamin align's Proust's work with dreamwork, suggesting that both emerge from the space between knowing and unknowing. Proust worked in the night so that he might better cling on to what Freud calls 'the web-like entanglement of the world of our thoughts' and what Benjamin calls 'intricate arabesques'. Benjamin tells us that come the morning we find these textiles fraying in our hands as we engage in the 'purposive' tasks of being alive. In other words, we have to forget our memories so that we can participate in the world we live in; isn't this a perfect description of alienation in a capitalist society?

This is why Proust sealed himself off; to avoid the alienating effect of the world outside. To make his web of remembering and forgetting his alone, and therefore to dwell much more intimately with the relationships that had formed him. Even alone in our bedlinen graves we are held in place by textiles made by other people. It seems to me that this is the contradiction of the interior: alone inside, we draw other lives closer to us than we ever do outside, but we are asleep to this intimacy. Blankets up to our chins, we take comfort in a web much larger than the one we are awake to.

*

When I was five we lived in Dundee for a year while my dad managed the opening of a branch of a bookshop and my parents' marriage ended. I remember helping my mother to untwist a hank of wool and put it on a swift to wind into a ball. A swift is a machine for winding wool; hers looked like an umbrella, it had arms that reached in all directions and folded in and out to guide the wool around and around.

My childhood was made from woven stuff, like the shawls my mum wore every day. There was a black one with yellow-gold edging, and a bright pink one, and a grey one with a straggly fringe. Sometimes I would get wrapped or covered or comforted with a shawl, at least when my little brother wasn't being carried in it. I re-member being embarrassed by the intimacy of sleeping on my teacher's cardigan folded up against the inside of the coach window on the way home from a school trip to a bird sanctuary. Comforted by a fabric that was not made to comfort me, a betrayal of my mother maybe.

We can consider the objects that children cling to through the lens of what the psychoanalyst Donald Winnicott called transitional objects and transition-al phenomena. In this theory Winnicott suggests that children form alliances with objects as they make the transition from the breast to the world at large. These 'not-me' objects are a child's 'first possession'. The arche-type is the blanket, sometimes the corner of a blanket making its way into the mouth along with a comforting hand, or a shiny label held in the hand or up to the face. These objects become conduits between parents, chil-dren, and other objects and other people in the not-me world.

When I first read Winnicott's case study 'String' in *Playing and Reality*, I recognised something. It is a case of a transitional object gone haywire. I feel for him, this seven-year-old boy who worried his parents by trying to tie all his furniture together with string: 'Whenever they went into a room they were liable to find that he had joined together tables; and they might find a cushion, for instance, with a string joining it to the fireplace.' Winn-icott felt that the boy was reacting to separation from his mother during times that she was hospitalised. The string, then, was an attempt to secure everything in the home in place, to bend it to his furious will. At one point he tried to incorporate his sister into his web by wrapping the string around her neck.

I don't remember a particular awareness of the dissolution of our family, perhaps because my father was absent much of the time anyway. But this desire to command the home and bring it under my control tugs on something I cannot quite find the end of. I asked Em about transitional objects when she called me to try and work out what was wrong with her television. She was knitting and she said that she couldn't change the channel and she could not bear to watch another episode of *Hetty Wainthropp Investigates*. She said I did not have a security blanket, she did not carry me in a shawl very much, that was more my brother; instead I wanted to be in the pushchair and to be able to look at things for myself. The only candidates she suggests for my transitional object were a small length of two-by-four which I carried for a while and then later a tape measure which I took with me everywhere. Apparently I would insist on measuring the objects in furniture stores and other people's houses. Trying to learn what objects were by learning their size. I was positioning each thing between me and the person holding the other end of the tape, holding them in place and imagining how I could exist at the other end of a table to them. Like the string boy, maybe I knew that furniture was a social object; if I could just learn everything about objects, I might be able to control people.

At the end of our year in Dundee I remember my parents walking around the henges they had made from piled cardboard boxes, inspecting them and marking them according to which home they would go to. Many years later my mum still occasionally remembers something that she had bought in a junk shop that my father took away.

Emily likes to rearrange the furniture. Sometimes when we were away visiting our dad, or out with friends, we would come back to find that she had moved improbably large things from one room to another. In her room is a large oak linen chest that she once moved from the ground floor of our terraced house to her upstairs bedroom. When it seemed that the nearby Thames was going to burst its banks one summer, she had us raise everything up on breeze blocks. This year she has decided she wants everything on the ground floor to be on casters. So far she has made one sofa, one table and one chest of drawers entirely mobile. Nothing can stop her from scooting from one end of the house to the other on her sofa. Dogs piled up beside her and with knitting on her lap, she can take herself anywhere she likes. I turned up recently in the summer and she was trying to persuade her partner to move the bed down onto the patio outside her back door so they could sleep outside underneath the wisteria.

A while ago I had to move home for a few weeks when I stopped really being able to be in the world. A breakdown and a break up had left me with nowhere sensible to live. But at home the house was in the process of being taken apart, every time I visited that year another wall had been removed, it was all being dismantled. A place where I wanted to feel certain about everything around me, but which Emily wanted to reconfigure totally. There I was, trying to understand my issues with abandonment and my inner child was simply not allowed to have the furniture where he wanted it to be. I could not have held it together with string or any other means. Which was worth finally learning.

*

I imagine that the string boy maybe used the rough brown string sometimes used in the garden, and sometimes to tie parcels. It is made of jute fibre, the twine that made Dundee rich and then poor when it went.

In response to the drug addiction that was endemic there in the nineties my brother's nursery school had the children make their own breakfast in the mornings so they could feed themselves if their parents were unable to do the necessary work. In the nineteenth century the jute industry had not been kind to children. They did not play with string but worked making it instead.

Jute is made from bast fibre that surrounds the stalks of two flowering plants from the genus *Corchorus*. The plants are still grown mostly in West Bengal in India and in Bangladesh. Beginning in the 1830s plants were imported to Dundee for processing, until rapid deindustrialisation in the 1980s meant that jute manufacturing was more or less gone by the time we lived there.

The plants grow quickly up to about four metres high. After they are harvested the roots are left in the ground to fix nitrogen for the next crop. The tall stalks of the plants must go through a process called retting. The stalks are submerged in pools of murky water where microbes help break down the outside of the stem, or the bast. This allows the fibrous material that makes up the bast to be stripped off, washed, and dried. Much of this work is still done by hand. The dried fibres are gathered in bundles and sold on to wholesalers. These look like long matted strands of golden hair.

There is a beautiful video on YouTube of a Chic Mitchell, 'born and bred in Lochee', speaking over footage of the men he used to work with unloading bales of jute from a truck. The film was shot in the 1980s, at the ragged end of the industry's life, and the narration was added in 2011. Chic, now an old man, dedicates the video to his friend Matt, now dead ('but his hook's still with me!' he says, brandishing the tool for heaving bales). 'Here's Geordie now, he's in a good mood.' 'He's hanging the teckle,' a line used to help lift the bales from the truck. 'This our first first load coming up now'; the truck backs into the warehouse and they begin to unload the bales, still looking like golden hair who knows how long after they were dried over poles in India. The narrator says: 'It's the only footage I've ever known of a stower carrying jute, I've never seen it before and you certainly will never see it again.'

In the 1830s the Dundee jute industry was spurred by a technical innovation: the fibre could be sprayed with an emulsion of water and whale oil to allow it to endure the machines that were used to spin and weave it. This is the reason that jute took root in Dundee; the city had a failing linen industry and a massive whaling fleet. At the height of the industry's success tens of thousands of people worked in the jute mills. Most of these were women and well into the twentieth century many were children. Children usually worked as shifters, removing full bobbins from the spinning frames and putting empty ones in their place.

One of the children working in the Dundee jute mills was Mary Brooksbank. A union organiser and a communist, Brooksbank is quoted as saying, 'I have never had any personal ambitions. I have but one: to make my contribution to destroy the capitalist system.' Aged fourteen she went on strike with other girls in the factory where she worked and secured a 15 per cent pay rise. Later she wrote a song called 'Oh Dear Me', a ballad of industrial exploitation, which you can hear her singing on a recording from the 1967 Festival at Blairgowrie.

> Oh dear me the mills gaein fast,
> And the pair wee shifters canna get nae rest;
> Shiftin bobbins, coorse and fine,
> They fairly mak ye wark for your ten and nine.
>
> Oh dear me I wish the day wis done,
> Rinnin up an doun the pass is nae fun;
> Shiftin, piecin, spinnin - warp, weft and twine,
> Tae feed an claith ma bairnies affen ten and nine.
>
> Oh dear me, the warld's ill divided,
> Them that works the hardest are the least provided;
> But I maun bide contented, dark days or fine,
> There's no much pleisure livin affen ten and nine.

These jute fibres were spun into a commodity chain which was strung from India to Dundee via the Arctic. Jute production was greased by exploitation and violence, workers and whales bound together in the pursuit of capital which would end up in the hands of the Jute Barons of Dundee. Nat Raha's 2021 poem in the magazine *Map* describes the whaling that took place in the Southern British territory of South Georgia:

> spring loaded innovative line
> *even the catcher would recoil by the gun*
>
> *– shoots in the footage –*
>
> cries when you axe it's life,
> becoming unit, becoming catch

It is the image of the recoil as the harpoon speeds from its gun to cut into the great body of the whale that makes me stop for breath. At that moment the whale is transformed: life 'becoming unit, becoming catch'. The poem is illustrated with a photograph from an archive held in Dundee: a photo of a blue whale being captured as part of the Discovery Oceanographic expedition 1925–27

The *Discovery* loomed large in my imagination when I lived in Dundee, a huge ship moored in the city that built it. It was famous for taking Scott to the Antarctic in 1901, and later it would carry out the first comprehensive survey of whale populations in the Antarctic around South Georgia. It was made by the ship builders who built the arctic whaling fleets that brought home the blubber that was rendered into oil to coat the jute fibres. I remember gawping at it: a real-life tall ship apparently made for adventure. As ever the fantasy of exploration and adventure for its own sake was only a smokescreen for colonial endeavour, the pursuit of more populations to destroy for profit. I wonder if the lines that secured the harpoons were ever made from Dundee jute?

In a city made by textiles I reached for the weft of the world in the woven. The hank of wool, the winder, the teacher's cardigan, the shawl. All of life is held in a net. It seems to me that Winnicott's string boy is using string to make visible the relations that hold together stuff and life. It is only later that we come to master the separation of self and other which we rely on to be in the world of adults. Mary Brooksbank was not long past the lessons of alienation that we learn as children before she had to strike for pay so that she could have more than ten and nine to take home. She learned the cruelty of a world ill-divided, and fought that alienation by binding herself to her fellow shifters and refusing to work.

It is for the sake of work that we accept the purposive action that Benjamin associated with forgetting our dreams. Cutting strings, letting go of blankets, distancing us from the others and the objects that we used to know are made of the same stuff as us. Maybe children have a kind of Marxist genius for the secret social life of the commodity. I suppose the question is whether the way we learn to live with objects is a condition of life, or only a condition of life under capitalism? It is notable that Winnicott calls the transitional object a child's first *possession*, a first commodity? Or perhaps the security blanket is a first act of political resistance.

*

Weaving, like dreaming, is always a kind of world making. The arduous task of setting the warp before starting work on a hand loom determines so much of what will be possible when the weaving begins.

Anni Albers, who made her career in the Bauhaus weaving workshop, wrote about 'the event of a thread'. The interlacing of one fibre with another at a right angle is an act of creation, it turns tangles of line into a complex and varied plane. In a small piece called *Pasture* made in 1958 Albers weaves a landscape from coloured cotton threads. Green, brown, cream, and orange – she makes a patchwork field of grasses, earth, and flowers. The most dramatic moments come when she escapes the immediate limits of warp and weft by twisting, knotting, and braiding threads that appear to defy the physical laws of her field in order to connect spots which are separated by the otherwise well disciplined parallel threads. A kind of quantum entanglement, from within the cosmos of the 35.6 x 39.4 cm rectangle, these knots must appear to be impossible magic.

Anni Albers makes universes. *Development in Rose I* (1952) is a cosmos with fewer dimensions than our own. It is an immense complexity straining to describe all it can within the limitations of warp and weft. Where threads twist together the resulting densities are like matter contorting the blanket of space and time. When the thread twists in one place the whole fabric responds, the tension registering in the warp like gravitational waves. A thin white net made from linen provides a geometrical background for two pale pinks and a sinister black thread to chase each other across the woven plane. The coloured threads take turns to grab onto one another to make twists and knots, and when they do so the pale wireframe underpinning this universe is momentarily visible. Each woven cosmos must take the form that it does because Albers has created the laws of physics which define them. She sets the rules. She chooses the materials which make up the periodic table. She is collaborating with the stuff of each weaving. Of course those cotton and jute fibres must twitch and scatter across the fabric of *Thickly Settled* (1957). Albers builds surfaces out of maths and touch. The light-absorbing black cotton is thrown into disarray by the brittle scratch of jute itching this way and that across the surface of this new land. Here the lines take on the rhythm of text, the etymological sibling of textile.

In *Haiku* and *Code*, two small studies from the early sixties, this link is made explicit: here a black thread runs through a weaving leaving dots and dashes and sinuous lines – what Maria Müller-Schareck, describing these pieces, calls 'an unknown encrypted script'. I think the link is less with the modern notion of text as a system of meaning, and more with the word as an object of creation and matter-making. In the beginning was the word – but maybe it is textile and not text that provides the best parallel for the genesis of the universe. Early in her career Albers wrote that weaving is 'the adventure of being close to the stuff the world is made of'.

While Albers knew that she was involved in a practice of creation she also knew that this work began at the scale of two threads crossing. She was convinced that weaving could play an integral part in the production of new ways of occupying interior space. Her diploma project at the

Bauhaus was a wall covering for an auditorium in a trade union school. The chenille, cellophane, and cotton fabric was designed with light and sound in mind. It was not attention grabbing but it would alter the room entirely. The double weave material at once softened the walls to sound waves and hardened them to light, the chenille and cotton creating a precise acoustic environment and the cellophane refracting and bouncing light back into the room.

T'ai Smith writes that 'what started out as a minimal, barely noticeable design at once filled and encased its environment.' Albers saw that woven materials were integral to the design of the interior. She recognised that the glass and steel boxes beloved of her architectural contemporaries were lost without an attentiveness to fabric. For the architect Philip Johnson's glass box guest house, built to extend the Rockefeller family's Manhattan mansion in 1950, Albers designed curtains woven from chenille and copper. In the daytime they would let the light in but at night they would create a more intimate space as the copper strands reflected the interior light, picking out the metallic flecks. Albers had a subtle mastery of textiles and she knew that it was a way to refigure the interior. For Albers weaving was, as Briony Fer has put it, 'a means to make work in which new ways of living could be articulated'.

Albers wrote an essay on weaving and architecture called 'The Pliable Plane': woven surfaces offer a much finer command of what comes in and what comes out of a space than a wall does. In 2018 some of her room dividers were displayed in a retrospective. Made in the late forties, Albers's dividers were based partly on Japanese screens. They were made from jute – in all likelihood spun in Dundee. The tough material was opaque enough that when densely woven it would be a baffle for light and sound.

I left the exhibition with fantasies of rooms and cities made of woven material. The pliable plane can be shaped to accommodate life. Life need not surrender wholly to these forgiving surfaces, bodies and textiles can reach a flexible accommodation, just as with the clothes we wear. There is still so much more that could be done with fabric to articulate new ways of living. Whether in the grand palampore of the nineteenth-century bourgeois apartment or the floral net curtain of a nineties suburban home, we already know that fabric is a way to carve out an environment for living.

I wonder if Albers ever wove with a thread that had been handled by Mary Brooksbank. Given the market share of the Dundee industry, it seems likely that some of the jute in Albers's work was at least made under working conditions that Brooksbank's strike helped to improve, or that the factory workers sang 'Oh Dear Me' as Albers's jute was twisted into threads and wound into balls using industrial-scale versions of the umbrella swift that I held for my mother in her studio in Dundee. Because the significance of the event of the thread is that it ties together the labour that manufactured it. Each weaving is a mass of social relations; the transformation of space and place within the woven is the product of hours of labour by maybe thousands of people. In the feeling of comfort I get when I sink into a sofa, pull over a blanket and hold on to a cushion I am embracing pure alienated labour – and it makes me feel so much better.

*

Blankets are a tool for survival, they are made to comfort and to protect us. Making a quilt, pieced together from scraps and patches, is a way of assembling life.

In the town of Gee's Bend, in Alabama, black women have been making quilts since before the abolition of slavery. Quilts were made from pieces of clothing or other domestic textiles; sometimes you can still see a leg or a sleeve. The art of quilt-making has been passed between generations over hundreds of years, and it has been a matter of survival and of resistance. Loretta Pettway Bennett, one of the Gee's Bend quilt makers, wrote:

> I came to realize that my mother, her mother, my aunts, and all the others from Gee's Bend had sewn the foundation, and all I had to do now was thread my own needle and a piece of quilt.

One of the earliest named quilt makers in Gee's Bend was Dinah Miller, who died in the 1930s aged 102. Miller had been kidnapped and transported across the Atlantic from the west coast of Africa in 1859, on a ship called the *Clotilda*, along with 110 other enslaved people. Piecing together scraps of scarce material, she stitched together quilts to keep herself and others warm.

The quilts came to national attention in the late 1960s when the area was reeling from evictions and job losses that were inflicted on the community in retribution for people registering to vote. The community formed a collective and signed contracts with Saks Fifth Avenue and Bloomingdale's. Their products brought in enough money not only to pay the workers in the cooperative but also to pave roads and bring electricity to the town. In Gee's Bend and in Alberta quilting has been a means to resist and to survive in a racist society.

The Gee's Bend quilters garnered attention from artists who were struck by parallels between their quilting and contemporary abstract painting. Lee Krasner visited and bought several quilts in 1967. The quilters' abstract compositions were compared with work by abstract expressionists. The quilters at Gee's Bend were making work in a tradition that stretched back to African and Native American textiles, and European artists have long scavenged for inspiration among the indigenous art of colonised places.

These blankets have been transformed into art by hanging them on gallery walls. Ella Bendolph's *Strips* (circa 1955) is made from pieces of clothing stitched together in vertical columns. Corduroy, wool, nylon, polyester, and cotton. Some patches preserve seams from the items they are made from: blue, check, purple, orange, brown. The pieces are all lined up but their different shapes create undulating vertical lines. The quilting runs diagonally across at a shallow angle creating ridges like in a ploughed field, or waves like on the Atlantic. These quilts have survived because they have been named as art, but millions of other blankets circulate with no maker's name attached to them.

A quilt made in Southern California by a woman called Mary Ann Beshers, who lived between 1918 and 1999, was worn on the Met Gala carpet by A$AP Rocky in 2021. The quilt was found in a thrift store by the designer Eli Russell Linnetz and incorporated into one of his collections as a garment. It was personalised for A$AP Rocky by Zak Foster who quilted a reverse for the vintage quilt made from red plaid fabrics, including a bathrobe owned by A$AP Rocky's dad. Only after the ball did one of Beshers's grandchildren recognise the design. Lives and memories and labour all made into an enormous embracing quilt which Zak Foster describes on his Instagram page as having 'soft bulk'.

I think A$AP Rocky knew the feeling of not wanting to stay inside and not wanting to go outside when he decided to hide his tuxedo inside an enormous quilt before going to a party. This is the magic of a blanket: it is an embrace you can carry, an interior which you can fold up and put in a bag, it will hold you just the same whether its maker loved you or not. It is its own kind of mobile home.

There was a quilt that my grandmother made that my brother and I used to fight over. It was made of square scraps of all kinds of material, lots of plaid and check, the binding was a faded red. We called it the Spaghetti Western quilt because my grandmother thought it seemed like something from the set of a Sergio Leone film. A quilt made for pioneers, for travel, for bringing the safety of home with you when you went out on the road to brutally colonise native lands. I was worried that it burned in the fire, but my brother says it is in Emily's mending pile at home.

When they are laid flat, quilts have a compositional beauty that draws the attention of those who seek to attribute to them the status of commoditised 'Art'. But when they are alive inside a home they do something far more expansive. Quilts are a way of creating an interior that describes life and not property. The blankets of Dutch sailors rounding the cape, the textiles of nomadic southern Africans perhaps traded for European goods before hostilities began, the pieces of cloth clung onto in the belly of Atlantic slave ships and referenced in generations of black quilting in Gee's Bend, the heavy curtains keeping out the drafts from my father's mother's parents' caravan, the quilt my mother made me: all these soft things are fragments of home transported and reassembled to make new interiors, even on the steps of the Met Gala ball.

And still we forget that the boundaries of the interior describe relations and thresholds between lives and landscape and not the ownership of a commodity – a grand fiction if there ever was one. We cling on to soft furnishings to stitch together a dream universe, an embrace to live in. I wonder what our homes would be if we thought of how to make them with weaving and stitches instead of bricks and mortar.

The Penelope work of forgetting. The weft that remembers and the warp that forgets. When the loving work of making a blanket has been performed by someone we know, it is easy to remember them as we feel the soft bulk of its embrace, but when it is performed by someone unknown to us they might as well have never existed. We forget the labour while we remember the feeling they imbued the commodity with. We remember our love of an object, while we forget what we owe to those who made it. Like in a dream we feel but do not know the things that tie together the objects we live among, a web of dependency that we quickly forget when we wake up and go to work. If as we snuggle into our bedclothes we were truly alive to the work which keeps us warm, we might wake up in a different kind of living room.

*

We ought to demand to be buried beneath the floorboards of our rented accommodation – to haunt the landlords forever.

In order to make room to live it will be necessary to remember all the ways in which life has already found its way into the interior. Every commodity in the home is an incendiary device that could yet be turned against the interests of capital, while each dwelling is a commodity, for someone, its value appreciating with no correlation to its capacity to nourish a good life.

I dream of a home where I can rearrange the walls, one that I can move to a location convenient to me. With no exchange value at all, it is merely and excessively a place for life. Galvey was almost a house like this; if you'd wanted to cut a hole in the wall you could have, I often thought about it and sometimes secretly tested this possibility with the tip of a compass. My grandmother, my mother's mother, wrote about her dream rooms in a novel called *Rhine Journey*. The main character, Charlotte, is a woman who has been trapped by Victorian patriarchy and class and who longs for an escape from expectation:

> she pictured to herself those whitened cottage rooms where she might quietly extend herself, and moving from room to room, meet and recognise herself in forms unaltered by the pressures of others upon her.

The interior can exert a pressure on our behaviour; such a dream could only be realised by escaping the bounds of the room and letting life constantly refigure our dwelling space. This is a utopia: moving from one room to another, being allowed to live in a place without second guessing oneself.

A sequence of rooms which are formed by oneself, not another's imagination of how you ought to live. Like a blanket, an interior which forms around your body, one which does not try to shape you in its own image. If only every person had an interior where they could extend themselves as they wish to. And were this to exist for all life then what a moment of revolutionary transformation this would be. No property, only space to live.

How does such a transformation of the interior take place? How can we eliminate the restrictions that the home as commodity places upon the way that we occupy the interior? It will surely come from the knowledge that we cannot escape the lives of others and we cannot choose whom we live with. The desire we have to draw things around us like a velvet coffin, like a bedlinen grave, is on the one hand a retreat from the world and on the other a desperate search for intimacy. In order to transform the home it will be necessary to understand that the comfort we find in our furnishings is the product of the labour of others.

We may be awake to the home as a fortification, as a fortress of solitude, but we are asleep to the dream of a collective life that is the wish from which the whole thing springs forth. Our lives are full of clues to this secret. How many home makeover shows see wealthy home-owners in one breath laud themselves for their magnanimous hosting and then in the next breath explain the extravagant cost of their open plan kitchen 'because we love to entertain'.

In their essay 'Naples' Walter Benjamin and Asja Lācis described the upturning of the logic of the bourgeois interior on the streets of Naples. They describe a city where one house fades into another and all homes spill into the public:

> So the house is far less the refuge into which people retreat than the inexhaustible reservoir from which they flood out... Just as the living room reappears on the street, with chairs, hearth and altar, so, only much more loudly, the street migrates into the living room. Even the poorest one is as full of wax candles, biscuit saints, sheaves of photos on the wall, and iron bedsteads, as the street is of carts, people and lights.

If we could take threads and draw lines between every interaction, every instant of collective joy, every borrowed utensil and every shared loaf, every overheard argument and every meal smelled in the stairways: imagine the beauty of this tapestry. When you open up your bed covers imagine yourself sleeping under such a blanket.

One of the great tricks of our society is to convince us that the ideal home is a castle. You can see the threat that this lie tries to see off in the life that flows out into the city in Benjamin and Lācis's description of Naples. Like a dream, a home is both individual and collective, its intimacy is drawn from its privacy and also the relations from which it stems. Allowing the home to be a commodity is not a gift of wealth but an impoverishment.

The job of a responsible capitalist is to stop every tendril from entering their masonry, to ensure that life leaves no trace. How much more would we have if our homes could extend out into the world, truly alive; if we could set our roots down into the foundations beyond the hard-edged containers that some have been able to eke out as possessions and others are forced to shelter within for a fee. Were it possible to visualise all the lines of relationship that extend out of the interior and into the world, then we would see the violence of severing such connections in order to protect the value of these commodities. Winnicott's string boy was trying to say this to his parents: if you go you will have to cut these strings which tie me to this home and to each of you. Do not commit this violence on me.

DENOUEMENT

Every good detective story ends with a denouement. The word comes from the French to unknot, to disentangle.

Inside Proust's cork-lined writing room there are documents and photographs pinned all over the walls. Between them are lines of red string tracing lines between drawing pins. There are so many points of convergence that the web has become a solid woven wall that further deadens the sound of the outside world. Only corners and edges of documents and images are now visible.

So you will have to take it on trust that I have found the purloined letter, and the latent content of the Wolf Man's dream, the Winter Garden photograph of Barthes' mother. I am standing here in front of you ready to reveal the secrets of the living room; you will find the outcome quite shocking. First we just need to disentangle the additional knots that have formed during our analysis.

The red threads have escaped the room. Through the windows and under the door they have crept into the hallways and out into the streets. This is a problem for us. One starts pinned to a scrap of William Morris wallpaper and ends in a tree in the Tuileries, another starts with a photograph of Mary Brooksbank and travels all the way to Dundee. This one extends all the way to Rue Daguerre and Varda's old apartment, this one goes to the site of block-printing workshops in Hyderabad where there is now a fifteen-floor apartment block filled with tech entrepreneurs. I'm getting distracted, suspended between sleeping and waking, inside and outside, held in a web of threads, embedded in a mad textile of interior life.

Time to call everyone into the parlour. Prepare the room for the entry of the great detective.

Cover the walls with chintz wall hangings and tapestries from Tudor courts. Mrs Hinch has been paid by a corporate sponsor to hoover up all of Proust's dust. We will need to transform the bed into a couch and cover the walls with picture frames. We will need a side table and a whatnot, an aspidistra and a Wardian case full of ferns. My grandparents' threadbare William Morris armchair will be resurrected from the ashes of their home, along with the seven foot sofa for a six foot loafer.

A velvet two-person couch – in green naturally – and an Anni Albers rug rolled out. A coffee table covered with figurines, potpourris, doilies, silver picture frames with pictures of the family, everyone in attendance. In the corner we will reconstruct Freud's desk, the monkey statuette, a letter opener, an ash tray, his signature round specs.

Next we will bring in the clues. A folded piece of paper with a coded message will prop up one of the uneven legs of a Windsor-back chair. A stolen letter will be inserted into the hollowed-out spindle of another chair. A footprint and a broken pane of glass next to the window. A blown up version of Daguerre's street scene, could that be a child at the window? A small cigarette burn on the velvet sofa, a scratch on the surface of the coffee table – how could that have happened with so many doilies to protect it!

A bird cage is brought in, it is made of fine metal painted with white lead paint, inside are four finches. When they have been set down on a side table, the door is opened and they are allowed to fly out into the room, free to perch anywhere they wish. Climbing ivy starts to make its way through the broken window (could the ivy be the culprit of this act of breaking and entering?); it moves quickly to cover one of the walls and starts to burst into incongruous flower like the tree of life. The birds leap from bough to bough pecking at fruit. In the tree across the street sit seven white wolves whose tails hang down in elegant curves.

The suspects process in, the copywriter from the Ikea advert, William Morris, Mrs Hinch (who has now realised the hoovering was a ruse). You are there too, and so is Judith Butler, Walter Benjamin, Edgar Allen Poe, my mother, father, me as a child, a cat with dirty paws, the landlady from *Keep The Aspidistras Flying*, Gracie Fields, Dinah Miller, A$AP Rocky, Rebecca, Agatha Christie, Agnès Varda, Bong Joon Ho and the cast of *Parasite*, Marcel Proust, Roland Barthes' mother, Barthes himself, Atget, Nadar; they keep arriving. As new people arrive the room is expanding, more seats appear, somebody brings out a tray of tea and biscuits. Here is Vivian and her mother, here comes Geordie, now he's in a good mood. Everyone is waiting for the arrival of the great detective, the landlord, the bengal cat, the psychoanalyst, the upholsterer.

Night is falling outside and the chenille and copper curtains are pulled across the whole length of the wall with the windows. The lacework of the doilies is sending out mycelia across the surfaces, the wall hangings are growing more and more fruits and flowers and they are falling onto the floor with thud after thud, the smell of violets everywhere as Mr Debroussian's trembling hands have dropped a large glass bottle of perfume onto the carpet. Someone unrolls another carpet on top to help mute the smell, and another, and another, until the carpets are piled so high in some places that people are having to stoop to avoid hitting their heads on the ceiling.

The interior is at breaking point, it is alive and its intentions are unclear. Sherlock Holmes arrives at the door and the room goes silent. He says that it was dastardly Capital all along, profit is the culprit, forcing each of us to retreat from the alienation of the outdoor world into our domestic compass cases. Forced by the delusion that the home is a space cut off from the world, each victim has enclosed themselves within a claustrophobic interior, numbed to the lives lived elsewhere. 'Look here,' he says, and pulls on a thread he finds behind a wall hanging. 'And look at this,' pointing towards a worn patch on an armchair, 'and here.' And then, drawing himself up to his full height, Holmes gestures vaguely at the people in the room and speaks with a raised fist: 'Take your magnifying glass to the clues in your own dream interior. Plant grass seeds in your carpet before you leave your next tenancy. Beneath the carpet, the earth!'

BIBLIOGRAPHY

A list of references is not the most effective way of pointing towards all of the writing and research which shaped *Living Rooms*. There are many more sources beyond those which I have drawn upon directly, but I have tried to be as comprehensive as possible. In order to avoid writing another entire book I have collected a list of sources as best I can below, by chapter, with repeats taken out.

OPENING

Attlee, Edwina. 2021. *Strayed Homes*

Freud, Sigmund. 2006. *Interpreting Dreams*. Trans. J.A. Underwood

Gornick, Vivian. 2015 [1987] *Fierce Attachments*

Proust, Marcel. 2003 [1913]. *In Search of Lost Time: The Way by Swann's* trans. Lydia Davis

CHINTZ

Fairs, Marcus. 2016. 'IKEA's "Chuck out your chintz" ads changed British taste, says the man who wrote the slogan' in *Dezeen* 2016

Hand, Michael. and Shove, Elizabeth., 2004. 'Orchestrating concepts: kitchen dynamics and regime change in *Good Housekeeping* and *Ideal Home*, 1922–2002'. *Home cultures*, 1(3)

Hardy, Barbara. 2006. *George Eliot: A Critic's Biography*

Isaac, Amanda C. 'Furnishings of the Chintz Room'. Website of Mount Vernon Estate

Jackson, Emily. 1900. *A History of Handmade Lace*

Kara, Siddhart. 2014. *Tainted Carpets*

Leslie, Deborah and Suzanne Reimer. 2003. Gender, Modern Design, and Home Consumption. *Environment and Planning D: Society and Space*. 21(3)

Marx, Karl. 2004 [1867]. *Capital*. Vol 1. Trans. Ben Fowkes

Metsger, Deborah. 2020. 'The Flowers of Indo-European Chintz' in *Cloth that Changed the World*. Ed. Deborah Fee

Morris, William. 1882. 'The Lesser Arts of Life' published in *Lectures on Art*

Morris, William. 1884. 'Art Under Plutocracy' in *Collected Works of William Morris, vol. 23*

Sykas, Philip. 'Refashioning Indian Chintz in the European Manner' in *Cloth that Changed the World*. Ed. Deborah Fee

Van Horn, Jennifer. 2018. 'An Indian Chintz Gown: Slavery and Fashion' in *The Junto: A Group Blog on Early American History*

VELVET

Benjamin, Walter. 2015. *Walter Benjamin's Archive*. Trans. Esther Leslie

Benjamin, Walter. *The Arcades Project*. Trans H. Eiland and K. Mclaughlin

Doyle, Arthur Conan. 1996. 'A Study in Scarlet' in *Sherlock Holmes: The Complete Stories*

Freud, Sigmund. 2004. Trans. J. Breuer. *Studies in Hysteria*

Gardiner, Muriel [and Sergei Pankejeff]. 1972. *The Wolf-Man and Sigmund Freud*

Spankie, Ro. 2015. *Sigmund Freud's Desk: An Anecdoted Guide*

Spinubzilla. 2020. [Twitter] 10 August

Textile Research Centre Leiden. 2019. VELVET! Digital Exhibition

PICTURE FRAMES

Atget, Eugene. 1992. Atget Paris

Barthes, Roland., 2009 [1980]. *Camera lucida: Reflections on photography*. Trans. Richard Howard

Benjamin, Walter. 2015. 'A Short History of Photography' [1931] in *On Photography*. Trans. Esther Leslie

Butler, Judith. 2004. *Precarious life: The powers of mourning and violence*

Butler, Judith. 2015. *Notes toward a performative theory of assembly*

Cox, Dan. 2020. 'The empty Streets (and parks) of Eugene Atget' in V&A Blog

Fischer, Molly. 2020. 'The Tyranny of Terrazzo: Will the millennial aesthetic ever end?' New York Magazine 2 March

Mayer, So. 2020. 'Daguerrotypes, Agnes Varda' on *Cinetopia Blog*, 18 August

Stanley, Bessie Anderson. 1905. In *Oxford Essential Quotations*, edited by Ratcliffe, Susan

Tsing, Anna Lowenhaupt. 2015. *The Mushroom at the End of the World*

Woodcraft, Saffron. 2020. 'Show Apartments As 'Aesthetic Traps': Risk, Enchantment And Illusory Homes In London's Olympic Park'. *Home Cultures*. 17:1

HOUSE PLANTS

Adams, Rachel. 2021. 'Home Grown' [exhibition]. Yoshimi Arts, Osaka. 30 January–21 February

Baines, Thomas. 1894. *Greenhouse and Stove Plants*

BOYD, Peter D.A. 1993. 'Pteridomania - the Victorian passion for ferns' in *Antique Collecting* 28 (6)

Harvey, W.F. 1933. *Moods and Tenses*

Keough, Luke. *The Wardian Case*

Oostenbrink, Phillip. 2018. 'Collecting Aspidistra', Thoughts of a Plant Nut.' [Blog] 4 May

Robinson, W. 1868. *Gleanings from French Gardens*

The Gardens Trust. 2018. 'Once the Queen of the Parlour'. [Blog] 22 September

Vislobokov, N. A. 2017. 'Flowering biology of Aspidistra (Asparagaceae): new data on pollination by dipteran insects' in *Plant Species Biology*. 32(4)

BLANKETS

Kohler, Barbara. 2007. *Niemands Frau*

Benjamin, Walter. 1999. 'The Image of Proust' in *Illuminations*. Trans. Harry Zohn

Winnicott, Donald. 2005. *Playing and Reality*

Hooly Dundee. 2011. *Dundee Jute Stowers – 1980s*. [Youtube] 24 December

Dundee Women's Trail. N.d. 'Mary Brooksbank' [website]

Mainly Norfolk. N.d. "The Jute Mill Song" [website]

Coxon, Ann, Briony Fer and Maria Muller-Scharek. 2018. *Anni Albers* [exhibition catalogue] Tate Modern London October 2018-January 2019

Smith, T'ai. 2014. *Bauhaus Weaving Theory*

Dinah's Legacy. N.d. 'Dinah's Story' [Website]

Freedom Quilting Bee Legacy. n.d. 'FQB artists' [website]

Beardsley, J., Arnett, W., Livingston, J. and Arnett, P., 2002. *Gee's Bend: The women and their quilts*

Walter Benjamin and Asja Lacis, "Naples" in *Reflections*. Trans. Edmund Jephcott

Raha, Nat. 2021. 'Blubber, Guts, Southern Leith' in *Map Magazine*. March 2021. [website]

Johnson, Rebecca May. 2019. *Unweaving The Odyssey: Barbara Kohler's Niemands Frau*

READING WALTER BENJAMIN

A reference on a page is not the best introduction to a text. In particular the extensive and sometimes cryptic bibliography of Walter Benjamin requires a little more explanation, I hope this book can encourage more people to explore his life and work. For an account of his life Esther Leslie's contribution to the Critical Lives series (2007 Reaktion Press) is excellent. His own beautiful autobiographical work *Berlin Childhood around 1900* [1932/8] is available from Belknap Press translated by Howard Eiland. The well-known collections of his writing *Illuminations* edited by Hannah Arendt, and *Reflections* edited by Peter Demetz are both essential. His essay with Asja Lacis, Naples, and his essay on Proust, both feature in *Illuminations* and are two wonderful texts with which to get to know Benjamin. Perhaps closest to the heart of this book are two of Benjamin's works: *One Way Street* and *The Arcades Project*. *One Way Street* was published first in 1928 and is a fascinating collection of fragments and aphorisms structured around objects and features of the everyday, it is available by itself in a lovely edition from Belknap Press (2016) and variously included in collections by Penguin and Verso. *The Arcades Project* is a work of mythic proportions, his plans for its publication are unclear. The text as it has been published is derived largely from papers which he secured with George Bataille before he fled Nazi occupied Paris. It was incomplete when Benjamin died by suicide in 1940. The text is a literary collage, made up of fragments collected under a series of alphabetical sections or convolutes. Of particular importance in this book was the section on the interior, as well as the two exposes from 1935 and 1939 – two versions of his summary of the project, specifically the sections on the bourgeois interior of the nineteenth century. More broadly his idea that the objects and commodities of modernity might reveal to us the dreams of a population has shaped my approach. *The Arcades Project* is an enormous project; it was published in English only in 2002 (Belknap Press) edited by Howard Eiland and Kevin Mclaughlin based on Rolf Tiedman's edited German edition. An essential guide to this text and a work of great critical insight on its own terms, is Susan Buck Morss' *Dialectics of Seeing* published in 1989 by MIT Press. There is much more beyond this to explore in Benjamin's work; his *Little History of Photography* written in 1931 is published in another lovely edition from Belknap Press as *On Photography* translated by Esther Leslie. Also translated by Leslie is the charming book *Walter Benjamin's Archive* published by Verso. Benjamin's work can appear to be hard work, but if you take the text on its own terms and not concern yourself overly with trying to decode it I think there is a huge amount of enjoyment to be found in his writing for any reader.

ACKNOWLEDGEMENTS

To everyone who has lived in and visited Galvey. Thank you to my family, you have taught me so much. Most of all to Nanny and Grumpy, to Emily, and to Kenza, all of your own creative endeavours are an inspiration to me in everything I do. To everyone else in my family, to my aunts and uncles, to my cousins (even Martha), thank you. We will all eat together at Galvey 2 soon!

I'm very grateful to everyone at Peninsula, particularly Will Rees whose work on *Living Rooms* has made it a better book in so many ways. Thank you also to my agent Imogen Morrell who always entertains my ideas.

I am indebted to so many teachers both at school and at university, those who have taught me and those who have been my colleagues. This book is larded with texts and ideas that I would never have known about were it not for you. In particular Jeanne Openshaw, Chris Pinney, and Andrew Harris.

So much of the thinking in this book has happened with and because of my friends. At lunch, in breaks at conferences, in pubs, and around our dinner table I have always been spoiled by friends who have taught me things. Edwina Attlee, for Sitting Room and Caff and Poetry Club and every conversation we have ever had. Phil Thomas, Matt Mahon, Sam Wilson, Harriet Boulding, and everyone else from LCCT and evenings at the Lord John Russell or the Bree Louise (RIP). Olivia Laing for weeding in the allotment and weeding in the text. Sophie Davidson for telling me to look happier when she took my author pic. Ben Critchley and Rachel Adams for reading *Capital* together with Rebecca and me, but also for watching *Blake's Seven* with me in 2005 and everything else since. For everyone else I have lived with or visited, this book is for all of your homes and all the tapestries that you are woven into.

Thank you most of all to Rebecca. You are the best reader, you teach me so much, and this book is full of ideas that came from conversations with you. Long live the book factory.